Waking Up to What You Do

Waking Up to What You Do

A Zen Practice for Meeting Every Situation
with Intelligence and Compassion

Diane Eshin Rizzetto

FOREWORD BY
Charlotte Jōko Beck

Shambhala
Boston & London
2006

Shambhala Publications, Inc.
Horticultural Hall
300 Massachusetts Avenue
Boston, Massachusetts 02115
www.shambhala.com

9 8 7 6 5 4 3 2

Printed in the United States of America

♾ This edition is printed on acid-free paper that meets the
American National Standards Institute Z39.48 Standard.

Distributed in the United States by Random House, Inc.,
and in Canada by Random House of Canada Ltd

Interior design and composition: Greta D. Sibley & Associates

The Library of Congress catalogues the previous edition of this
book as follows:
Rizzetto, Diane.
Waking up to what you do: a Zen practice for meeting every
situation with intelligence and compassion/by Diane Rizzetto.
p. cm.
ISBN 1-59030-181-1 (hardcover: alk. paper)
ISBN 1-59030-342-3 (paperback)
1. Religious life—Zen Buddhism. 2. Buddhist precepts. I. Title.
BQ9286.R59 2005
294.3'444—dc22
2004023928

The thought manifests as the word;
The word manifests as the deed;
The deed develops into habit;
And the habit into character.

So, watch the thought and its ways with care
And let it spring from love
Born out of concern for all Beings.
As the shadow follows the body,
As we think, so we become.

—The Buddha, from the *Dhammapada*

CONTENTS

Contents

FOREWORD

Anyone who takes Diane's book to heart has a great opportunity to open a door to understanding the Buddhist precepts. This book, however, is one to be read carefully and thoroughly because opening the door to the precepts has to be done with intelligence. Without intelligence and a constant awareness of our beliefs about life and ourselves, the precepts remain closed and may be viewed as a set of rules—Thou Shalt Nots—which can be harmful.

By all means, this book should not be construed as a Thou Shall Not presentation, and Diane covers the possibilities where misinterpretation of the precepts and their functioning can occur. This is a book about choice, responsibility, and being awake to the motivation and consequences of our actions. We all must engage in events as they unfold in our lives; we have a choice, however, to do this with either intelligence or ignorance. The precepts presented here are guidelines to help us tap the intelligence within us. For anyone who is serious about considering their actions, much benefit can accrue from the study of the precepts offered here.

The book deals honestly with Diane's own life—her early struggles, her Zen practice, and how her use of the precepts in her life taught her that the responsibility for how one deals with the difficulties in one's life rests in one's own choice of action. It is warm, clear, attractive instruction.

I urge you to travel this road along with Diane, considering carefully the fundamental question the precepts ask: What prevents you from living the way you want to live your life? In this journey the precepts ultimately reveal with crystal clarity the truth that our happiness and well-being is intricately connected with the happiness and well-being of others.

—Charlotte Jōko Beck
San Diego, California 2004

PREFACE

There's a rumor going around that if you stick with it long enough, a book will begin to write itself. Taking that proverb on faith, since this is my first book, I kept a diligent eye for the smallest sign of little nubs developing along the edges of my thoughts—nubs that would finally bud into little fingers whose job would be to effortlessly carry my thoughts into the writing of this book.

Maybe that works for some folks but not even the slightest swelling of a nub appeared for me. I finally gave up and settled for the fingers I've got—sometimes hesitant, uncertain, and searching and sometimes strong, decisive and sure. Natalie Goldberg says we need to "carry the [writing] away from the desk and into the kitchen." I, however, have found that I needed to carry the kitchen into my writing. So the fingers that wrote this book are the same that fumbled their way through my teenage pregnancy, dropping out of high school, a difficult first marriage, single parenting, and finally tapping their way into Zen practice and teaching. The book didn't write itself. What wrote it were my own life experiences and the experiences of my Zen students with whom I have been honored to share the practice.

The subject of this book is the Buddhist precepts. But perhaps more precisely it is a book about choice, responsibility and being awake to the motivation and consequences of our actions. Whatever language we speak, whatever social/cultural background we have inherited, and whether we follow a spiritual path or not, we all must engage in events as they unfold in our lives. We have a choice, however, how we do this. The precepts presented here are guidelines to help us tap the intelligence within all of us.

How I work with my Zen students, however, is not exactly the same as what is presented in this book. For one thing, our work takes place mostly one-to-one. I do not teach specific precept classes, and most group discussions occur during one of my Dharma talks. I also do not ask my students to explore the precepts in any particular order. After looking them over, the student picks one that she feels she often struggles with. We begin with that one and then move through the remainder in the same manner. Oftentimes after working on one precept, the next will follow quite naturally. Over the years, it has been my experience working in this way that an order similar to what's presented in this book more or less reveals itself. So I begin with the precepts related to speech: speaking truthfully and speaking of others with openness and possibility. The discussion in this book is aimed at presenting an overview of what my one-on-one work might look like, and offering the reader an opportunity to explore the possibility of taking up this type of inquiry with a qualified teacher.

I usually suggest that people wait until they've had some experience with practicing mindfulness meditation before they take on the practice of precepts focus. I suggest this because it's helpful before they work with the precepts to develop some ability to sit in stillness with awareness of the thoughts, emotions, and sensations occurring in the body. It usually takes a year or so for this awareness to develop. Secondly, I want them to have the tools to experience that awareness in their daily life—when they're off the meditation cushion. Finally, I offer them ways to focus that awareness on specific behaviors such as the ones the precepts cover. For readers who have not had experience with a meditation practice, I suggest you follow the instruction presented in "A Primer in Awareness Practice" at the end of this book to get started, and then, in time, contact a teacher with whom you can have some feedback in your practice.

ACKNOWLEDGMENTS

I offer appreciation to my teacher, Charlotte Jōko Beck, who continues to be a source of inspiration to me, to Sojun Mel Weitsman for his guidance in my early years of Zen practice, and to my Zen students whose insights have found their way into these pages and with whom I have the honor to share this practice. I also thank my family and all those who have helped through the various stages of writing this book. Finally, my deep appreciation to my husband, Jay, who so often serves as my lighthouse.

Waking Up to What You Do

A Sink Full of Teaching

For the years my husband and I worked in our home offices, our meeting place was our kitchen sink. Well, not that we made appointments to meet each other in front of the sink and faucet, but it's where the dishes we individually used throughout the day met. My office was on the second floor and his office was in the basement of our house. The kitchen was in the middle. A good part of a day would pass when the only indication that the other was present in the house was what was left in the kitchen sink after we would each at different times go there to make a cup of tea or coffee or to get a quick bite to eat.

One day, I began to notice that every time I went downstairs to the kitchen, another dirty dish or two appeared in the kitchen sink. At first this didn't trouble me. It was just another dish in the sink. But as the day went on, I found that I was counting the number of dishes and separating them into *his* dishes and *my* dishes. On one or two visits to the kitchen, I even washed my dishes and let his remain. And with each trip to the kitchen, I added to the dishes in the sink another thought about these dishes. Many thoughts collected about his dishes that he just leaves there expecting me to clean up. What makes him think my time is expendable and his not? Greater and greater the story grew, and without my really knowing it, the sink became filled with far more than the dirty dishes.

Then on one occasion, as I was making a cup of coffee, my husband appeared in the kitchen. "Hi," he said.

Silence.

"Could you make a cup of coffee for me too?"

Silence.

"Could you. . . ." Cabinet door slams. With an indignant reaction, I indulged my anger and stomped off to my office leaving a bewildered husband standing in the kitchen in front of a sink full of dirty dishes.

A sink full of dirty dishes, getting cut off in line at the grocery store, or any other encounter we have from day to day might seem a little too ordinary for a book that talks about Buddhist precepts. But, it is our reactions to these seemingly unimportant situations we face in our daily lives that make up our worldviews and show our true colors. Even a small incident like my experience at the kitchen sink can send us into a tailspin. Within a few seconds, we've gone from a simple encounter to a raging argument. In the heat of the anger, both sides hurl off insulting words and it seems that the sole intention is to hurt one another.

In time, things might cool down enough to leave just the reverberations of our angry actions. After the storm, feelings of guilt, sadness, and hurt might surface. Thoughts to never to do it again might arise. Or perhaps along with the outburst arose feelings of strength, self-righteousness. Perhaps the reactive behavior gets blamed on conditions or others. Maybe there's a combination of guilt and blame. Whatever the reverberation, remorse or anger, one reaction has just moved to another and another. After I answered my husband's simple request for a cup of coffee by barging off to the solitude of my office, the thoughts that blamed him began to turn toward myself. "You're taking my important time from me so that I can wash the dishes you dirtied" became, "What kind of person am I to think this way? I'm not worth much if I can't even wash the dishes without getting angry or feeling taken advantage of."

You can fill in your own most recent story about something that triggered words or actions that got you worked up. Notice what you did after the dust settled. If you didn't take time to question deeply what was going on with you during the incident, then you can be assured that what you did afterwards was react. It seems, then, in order to see things more clearly, we need to be able to see when we've strayed into reactive thinking. Only then do we have a chance to take action that best suits the conditions present at any given time and that best serves the situation. This is how the precepts can be of help, serving as a tool for waking up to our reactive thinking. We don't just think about ourselves, but consider the impact of our actions and words on the people and things around us. We don't think only of what would make us happy, but also include in our choice of action the well-being of others.

My Own Story

Zen practice sort of snuck up on me from behind. After dropping out of high school in 1959 (my junior year) I had little understanding or interest in anything but taking care of my babies, who arrived eighteen months apart, and trying to keep an ill-fated marriage from falling apart. The passion for Eastern religions, particularly Zen, which began to take hold in the United States during the early 1960s, escaped me completely. I lived a stone's throw from the burgeoning counterculture of Harvard Square and the Cambridge Zen Center, but I may as well have lived tucked away in a small town. I had never even read a book from cover to cover, let alone a Zen book! My world was pretty much limited to soap operas, romance magazines, washing diapers, and figuring how I was going to pay the rent each month. Several years later, as a single mother and after a short period on the welfare rolls, I found whatever jobs a high school dropout could land—a factory worker, nightclub hostess, or barmaid—in order to support myself and my children. I soon figured out that prospects would be pretty dismal if I didn't get some education. I returned to school hoping to just get my high school diploma and perhaps get a decent job as a secretary. But it didn't work out that way, thanks to Mr. Sheldon Daly, a Boston lawyer.

I lied my way into Mr. Daly's office after I read in the newspaper's classified section that he was hiring a legal secretary to run his office. By now I had taken the necessary courses to earn my high school certificate, but my office skills were far from what the job required. Nevertheless, I managed to convince him that I really could type and take shorthand a lot better than I demonstrated in my interview. I even arranged for him to call for references from a friend who would back up my story. He believed my story and hired me.

It wasn't long before it became clear to him that I was making a mess of things, and that I had lied to him about my skills. One day, he sat me in his office and said, "Look, this isn't working out. I don't want to hear about why you misrepresented yourself when I asked for your qualifications, but what I do want to hear about is how you would like your life to be five years from now. What kinds of choices do you think you need to make to make that a reality?" The question left me dumbfounded. Not only was he telling me to *get a life,* but he was also saying that I had an option to choose what my life could be.

Today, what resounds even more for me is that Mr. Daly looked beyond what most other bosses consider their prerogative. He was more interested in how he could help me than how he could judge me. By not seeing me through my faults, Mr. Daly engaged in what I have called the precept of *meeting others on equal ground.*[1] In doing so, he gave me the freedom of choice and gently, but directly, reminded me that the responsibility for how I deal with difficulties in my life rests in my own choice of action. This implicit responsibility is at the heart of what I would like to offer the readers of this book about the precepts.

Like a good Zen riddle, Mr. Daly's question wormed its way into my psyche, forcing to the forefront of my thinking possibilities that I had only dreamed of in the past. When I met with him again, I told him I wanted to go to college and to perhaps become a teacher. That's all he needed to hear. He got on the phone, made a few contacts, and within several months I found myself attending night school as a college freshman. By his willingness to put aside my dishonest behavior, Mr. Daly had again engaged in the precept of *meeting others on equal ground.* It was this early, unconscious experience of the power the precepts have that I rediscovered later when I began to practice Zen.

Seven years later my life had made a complete turnaround. I had finished college and graduate school, married my current husband of thirty-five years, and was in the midst of parenting adolescents. I had heard a little bit about Zen Buddhism because by now, Harvard Square bookstores were among my haunts. But I had never read any Buddhist books even though my husband had already started to do some reading on his own.

One late night I was anxiously pacing the floor waiting up for one of my teenage children to return home from a party. I paced the room, thinking about all types of worst-case scenarios, when my eye caught a book lying on the table that my husband was reading. Just trying to get my mind off of my worries, I opened it and thumbed through the pages. I read: "Strictly speaking, for a human being, there is no other practice than this practice; there is no other way of life than this way of life." The book was Suzuki Roshi's *Zen Mind, Beginner's Mind*.[2] As I think of it now, there it was again—another reminder to look at my life because that is all there is.

It might seem that my next stop would be the closest Zen center, but not so. Life's lessons continued to sneak up from behind. I had a good job as a high school English teacher, a wonderful husband and children. Everything I had worked hard to achieve was materializing, and yet there seemed to be deeper questions lurking. There were things that were not yet resolved, such as my relationship with my mother from whom I had become estranged.

After moving to California in the late 1970s, I was once again prompted by my husband's interest in Zen. I found my way to the Berkeley Zen Center. When I walked in the door to the meditation hall, I felt that I had walked into a forgotten home. It seemed natural and right. Zen practice had finally caught up with me.

Over the next few years, I immersed myself in Zen practice, meditating mornings and evenings, attending many retreats, reading, and studying. I took the precept vows in the Buddhist ceremony of Jukai. This is a ceremony in which lay Zen practitioners may participate as they deepen their commitment to Buddhist practice. These are the precepts that I will discuss throughout this book: Not Taking Life, Not Indulging in Anger, Not Stealing, Not Gossiping, Not Putting Oneself above Others, and Not Using Substances to Cloud Awareness. Nevertheless, the sense that I was missing something crucial continued to nag at me.

I understood in an intellectual way the teachings of wisdom and compassion—trying to live a life that is not harmful to others. There were times when I experienced very deep moments of openness and peace. But even though I took up the precepts as vows to engage only in action that is compassionate, to let go of anger, to forgive and not judge others, it was still impossible for me to even consider engaging in this kindness and forgiveness with my own closest kin—my mother. I could not bring myself to pick up the phone and call her, three thousand miles away. The four years of silence, harboring anger, hurt, and resentment, made hearing her voice too great a source of dread. In taking the precepts I had vowed to not indulge in anger and to not view others through a lens of fault. But those vows were only words stuck to my tongue. They hadn't yet made it to my heart.

So I, the diligent Zen student, learned that I could be open, giving, and caring around the Zen center, but in some fundamental way, my heart was closed. I asked myself, How can I continue in assuming that I am keeping these vows unless I face the truth about this silent distance? I was so angry at the perceived injustice of my mother's actions that, contrary to the precept, I continued to indulge in that anger. It consumed me so much that I could only see her through a lens of fault. It would be nice to think that the next step in my practice was simply picking up the phone and dialing my mother's number, connecting with her from across the continent, California to Boston. But it wasn't.

In fact, it was over a year before I mustered up the courage to take that first step toward unraveling the beliefs and assumptions that harbored the anger and guilt of all those years. And it took even more years after that to uncover the layers of fear. It wasn't until then that I began to understand that the precepts weren't simply vows to not take actions, speak words, or think thoughts that were hurtful, but that they could lead me to grapple with essential questions in my daily life, such as why I couldn't dial my mother's telephone number. With this realization, the precepts began to stir deeply within me.

Today, the understanding that meditation practice is an everyday part of our relationships is fairly common. Nevertheless this understanding doesn't make what we have to eventually face any easier. We have to face our demons and our disappointments. There is no designated time or place for doing this. As long as we are practicing earnestly, practicing with a sincere effort to face the truth about our lives, sooner or later a light will go on and we'll say—perhaps with a shudder or a sigh—"Oh, this is a crossroad. Maybe, instead of launching into my usual defensive manner of dealing with avoiding the phone call to my mother, I'll hang back and see if there's a bit of something I can learn here."

If we engage in trying to understand our actions, then something begins to change. For example, in the experience with my mother, over several months, I had thought from time to time about making contact with her, but every time the thought arose, the butterflies fluttered in my stomach, my breath shortened, and I quickly drove the possibility from my mind. Then, one morning, instead of ignoring the dread of the phone call, I sat by the phone and gave myself permission to witness whatever came up. At times I experienced dread, other times anger, sometimes righteous indignation, and other times deep sadness. I performed this ritual many times. Each encounter with the phone dial brought me closer to truly understanding the meaning of the precept *I take up the way of letting go of anger.*

As I replayed the same old story that made me the victim, I learned that just under the rising heat of anger was the quickening heartbeat of the fearful child. Sometimes I wanted to forget it all and lapse into the story of why I didn't have to face any of it—why the silence was justified. Then I began to learn something about the precept of *I take up the way of meeting others on equal ground.* Maybe I didn't speak ill about my mother or gossip about her to others, but certainly I was invested in blaming or faulting her. Round and round I tumbled, until I finally began to experience the sinews of my resistance loosening. I engaged in this ritual over many months before I finally picked up the receiver and dialed Boston—617. . . .

I found later as a Zen teacher that what took me years to stumble into can be more directly accessed by working with the precepts: the knowledge that understanding of useful action emerges from the most ordinary events of everyday life and in the situations we want to avoid most. This is the approach to the precepts upon which I base my work with my students.

There is no rule or formula that can tell you what to do. There is no calculation that you can always perform that will determine the best course of action for every situation. But one thing we can rely on is that if we learn how to be present in the situation without getting caught in self-centered thinking, our chances of taking action that best serves the situation will be far greater. This is where working with the precepts as an awareness practice can be of help. Sometimes the way will be clear and sometimes not. If it's not, you just make the best choice you can and practice with the results.

So we can think of the precepts both as keys to self discovery, allowing us to see how our habitual patterns of
thinking lead us to do things that are hurtful to ourselves
and others, and as companions signaling us when we are
about to take hurtful action. They encourage us in the
spirit of open questioning to unveil our deepest beliefs that
define for us the shape and limitations of how we view who
we are. They reveal with crystal clarity the truth that our
happiness and well-being are intricately connected to the
happiness and well-being of others; we can't have one without the other. In the deepest sense, our actions are our her-
itage let go into the world.

PART ONE

ONE

What Are the Precepts?

The Buddhist precepts came about originally as rules to govern the community of monks and nuns who gathered together to realize a life not dominated by senses, feelings, emotions, and thoughts. The precepts they followed included very precise instructions for daily encounters—such as not handling money, not eating certain foods, and not touching people of the opposite sex—and were intended to support the monks and nuns in their monastic practice. Later, as Buddhism spread into lay communities, the precepts were broadened to include people who had not undertaken such austere forms of practice. Today, the precepts are also taken by people who live their lives driving the freeways, doing time in prisons, and changing baby diapers. For some, the precepts are viewed as a preliminary step in becoming a Buddhist practitioner. For others they are taken only for the duration of a meditation retreat. In the Zen tradition, taking the precepts is made formal in the ceremony of Jukai, in which a student is initiated as a lay Buddhist practitioner. *Jukai* is from the Japanese, and means to *receive* the precepts. The form of the precepts reflects time, place, and the conditions present, and they vary slightly from tradition to tradition. Nevertheless, their essence remains constant.

A Beacon Light

A precept can be thought of as a beacon of light, much like a lighthouse beacon that warns sailors that they are entering dangerous waters and guides them on course. It can show us the way but also it warns us to Pay Attention! Look! Listen! Sometimes we will change course, other times, if we must reach shore, we will proceed with caution. Say for some time, you've been considering ways in which you take what is not freely given to you, and one day you're standing in line at the supermarket and notice a twenty-dollar bill on the floor by your foot. You bend over to pick it up, thinking, I can easily take this for myself without anyone noticing. Then you remember the precept *I take up the way of taking only what is freely given.* The precept signals to watch yourself: Pay Attention! Look! Listen! So instead of pocketing the twenty-dollar bill, you take in the person in front of you as part of the whole picture, and you ask if she's dropped some money. Your action considers and therefore responds to much more—the person who dropped the twenty dollars, their families or friends, and the other people in the line.

The precepts are offered and received as tools to help free us from domination by the ever-changing stream of thoughts, feelings, and sensations. They mirror and guide us through our strongest desires, our deepest fears, our greatest accomplishments. They turn awareness toward the ebb and flow of our personal physical and psychological experiences. They're like a firm but compassionate hand on the shoulder that points to the unending dance of cause and effect that helps us understand that no result comes about completely independently. The apple I had with lunch came about because of the seed within its core with the design of apple in its genetic structure. Together with the soil, water, and sun, *apple* comes into shape—round, red, tart, and juicy. How it finds its way into my mouth comes about because of the hand that picked it from the tree, the truck that was driven to the supermarket, and on and on. Can we pinpoint one cause, one effect? We can only know that in every seed there is a fruit and that in the words of Ralph Waldo Emerson, "the end preexists in the means." It would do us well to consider this carefully when we choose to take hurtful action. Used skillfully, the precepts can, pebble by pebble, boulder by boulder, bring down the walls of separation and reveal our connection to loved ones and enemies alike. They reveal our connection to not just people and animals, but to the blade of grass under our foot, the river filled with plastic bottles and chemicals, the delicate sway of ecological balance, our leaders who bring us in and out of war and declare our nations' friends or foes. They reveal the ways in which we fall into vicious cycles of thinking and acting, causing suffering to ourselves and others. They are never intended for us to view these actions as moral defects but rather as the root or source of suffering.

A Sign above the Door

You might also think of a precept as a sign above a door that reads "Enter Here." As I sat silently in front of my office desk after storming out of the kitchen with the sink full of dirty dishes, the sign above my door read *I take up the way of letting go of anger*. It was an invitation to enter and explore. The Enter Here sign signals a point of entry from which we can begin to explore more deeply our habitual patterns of thinking, feeling, and acting. These patterns have been deeply ingrained into our daily lives. The precept invites us to enter and to meet the intention of our actions open and honestly, thus gaining access to some of our most difficult issues. It is not a directive to berate ourselves for our behavior, but to face squarely the consequences of our actions on ourselves and others.

To enter the exploration of a precept can be a scary move for some of us, and we may try to find all types of ways around it, but it helps to take whatever tiny steps we can to meet ourselves squarely. So when we find we've lied about something to cover a mistake we made at work, or we didn't speak up when we could have clarified the truth, the precept of speaking truthfully reminds us that this is our point of entry. This is the doorway through which we must pass if we are to truly know and be at peace with ourselves.

A Riddle

The precepts are also a riddle of sorts, an unsettling question that denies us easy answers. Is it always wrong to lie? How do we live our lives without killing? What happens when the rules fail and the answer isn't clear? There is an old Zen riddle that goes something like this:

> You're sitting in the forest when you see a rabbit run by. A moment later, a hunter comes up to you

and asks if you've seen a rabbit. If you answer "yes," you will indirectly contribute to the death of rabbit. If you say "no," you break the precept not to lie. What can you do? Most of us figure it would be better to save the rabbit and break the precept about lying. But, what if you see three hungry children following the hunter? Then what would you do?

How do we solve this riddle? How do we solve the question of whose responsibility it is to wash the dishes in the kitchen sink? This riddle is no trick question challenging us to come up with an enigmatic answer. Rather, it intentionally stumps us as a way of challenging our usually prescribed answers about when it's right to do this or that. It places the responsibility for action directly where it belongs—in our ability to see and respond to events and situations with clarity and intelligence.

Should/Should Not

Engaging them skillfully, we find the precepts are tools of discernment encouraging us to take action that arises out of clear seeing. Unlike commandments or rules by which we judge ourselves, they prod us to wake up and see clearly the reality of each and every situation and to take appropriate action accordingly. The precepts can also be described as keys that, if used skillfully, can help us unlock the closets we don't want to open—closets that hold what we don't want to face and closets that hold our deepest potential. They can point us toward exploring the moment when things aren't the way we want them to be. They are aspirations that help us take appropriate action. I view the precepts as tools that help us turn inward, unlocking our deepest human capacity for love, empathy, fairness, and joy. These are traits that can be found in our most ordinary, everyday living. The precepts direct us not toward an abstraction with which we measure our self-worth, but they engage us in action that reveals all the goodness we are capable of in ordinary, everyday situations, including our disappointments.

The precepts also remind us that our actions are sometimes fueled by the desire to serve only ourselves, often at the expense of others. It's what we often do: we think self-centered thoughts, and we act on them. Blaming or hating ourselves for this is of little use. What can be of great use, however, is to acknowledge that to err is human and that wisdom and compassion are not limited to the gods. This is a first step toward identifying and letting go of the defenses that stand in the way of our taking the actions that spring from our connections to one another. To act in this way, of course, is not always so easy, so we look to the precepts as *fundamental human values* for guidance. Committing ourselves to explore and abide by these human values can be a way to remind us of what we so easily forget when we're scared or angry: that we can never take action that does not affect everyone, including ourselves.

The Precepts

- I Take Up the Way of Speaking Truthfully.
- I Take Up the Way of Speaking of Others with Openness and Possibility.
- I Take Up the Way of Meeting Others on Equal Ground.
- I Take Up the Way of Cultivating a Clear Mind.

- I Take Up the Way of Taking Only What Is Freely Given and Giving Freely of All That I Can.
- I Take Up the Way of Engaging in Sexual Intimacy Respectfully and with an Open Heart.
- I Take Up the Way of Letting Go of Anger.
- I Take Up the Way of Supporting Life.

For those of you familiar with the traditional order of the Buddhist precepts, you will note that they are worded and ordered a little differently from how you might expect.[1] However, if you are interested in following a more traditional order, there are many excellent sources by contemporary teachers. The order I have chosen is that which most accurately reflects the one most commonly discovered by my students. Because this book is for a general audience, many of whom will have no experience or knowledge of formal awareness practice, I have also chosen to discuss just eight of the traditional ten prohibitory Zen precepts. The other two precepts—Not Sparing the Dharma Assets and Not Defaming the Three Treasures—the reader will notice are nevertheless discussed indirectly within some of the other precepts. When my students study the precepts with me in person, we include all ten of the Zen precepts.

Voicing the Vow of the Precept

There are several ways in which a person may express her intention to live her life wholeheartedly from within the guidelines of the precepts. Over the years, and especially with the writing of this book, I struggled with the question of whether to phrase them as prohibitions or as aspirations.

As a Prohibition

As a prohibition, the precept is expressed as a vow to re-frain from a specific action—"I *vow* to not take what is not freely given," or "I *take up the way* of not taking what is not freely given." This form can be useful in providing clear parameters for our behavior. It is meant to support us and keep us on track when we stray into muddled thinking.

Some time ago, after using my credit card to pay for some purchases in a store, I walked out of the store without checking the receipt. Halfway down the block, I took a look and noticed that I was charged seven dollars for a seventy-dollar purchase. The store clerk had made a typo and the number 0 was missing. Within five seconds I watched my mind do a jig as thoughts arose: Oh, oh, a mistake. I could just keep walking. Who'll know? I'd save myself sixty-three dollars. Then the precept entered: Wait a minute, that's tak-ing what's not freely given. You have to go back. So I did. The direction was clear and prohibitive—*don't steal!*

As an Aspiration

Another way to voice the precept is as an aspiration: *I take up the way (or vow) to take only what is freely given and give freely of all that I can.* In this case, the emphasis is on what we aspire toward, instead of what we try to refrain from. I have chosen to use this type of wording in this book because I think it more accurately expresses the spirit in which I work with the precepts—as pointers, directing us toward our natural propensity to take action out of love and concern for one another. Secondly, when voiced in the pro-hibitive form, it seems more likely that we will rely on them as an *outer* authority that judges and keeps score. Lastly, it has been said that the best way to learn something new is by doing it. Although I am not suggesting that we simply change our behavior without some insight into what's behind it, I have found that the best teacher is what we experience when, for example, we give freely all that we can.

After my students have explored a particular precept for some time and have developed some clarity around their behavior, they voice the precept in their own words. For example, one student who was practicing with the precept *taking only what is freely given and giving freely of all that I can* voiced it this way:

> *At times when I feel I am entitled to what others want, need, or own, I resolve to hold this hard ball of entitlement, of separation, to feel its texture, and to wait until its nature is clear before taking action.*

Over the years, I have found that as I go through this process with my students, revisiting the precepts myself, the wording has deepened along with my understanding of the ways the precepts play themselves out in my own experience.

The precepts encourage us to go beyond the *just don't do it*. They invite us to willingly grapple with the slipperiness of what's the best action to take given the circumstances of any given situation. They direct us toward considering what conditions are present here and now. Sometimes the best thing to do is lie. Sometimes it's best not to lie. It's not so hard a decision if a lie will clearly save the lives of innocents. But what about the more difficult times when the water grows muddy, and we're not so certain? When we take up the way we accept the uncertainty as part of our lives and return to open inquiry into our actions, from moment to moment, day to day, year to year. So I have chosen to express the precepts as much as possible from aspiration—from the strength, caring, and clarity that reveal themselves when we come to know our *selves* intimately.

I Take Up the Way: The Vow

We may have all types of ideas about vows or taking vows. But a vow is simply a heartfelt intention to be open, honest, and responsible. *Intention.* That is the key to the vow. Although you may not necessarily be taking a formal vow to take up the way of a precept, it is useful to discuss a little about what it means to make this type of commitment.

Recently, I attended a wedding ceremony in which the couple took the precepts as part of their vows. I overheard a young man standing close by say, "Whoa! There's no way I could commit to all that stuff!" This is not an unusual re-action even after my own students have decided that working through the precepts is a direction they want to take in their lives. Some of them become a little queasy around the idea of taking a vow. They may think, What if I can't do it? Or sometimes they feel they may be scrutinized by those close to them every time they have a glass of wine or chill out by watching TV, wondering, Will people think I'm using sub-stances to cloud my awareness? Vows are not useful when we use them as yardsticks to measure ourselves and others, thinking, I don't gossip about others the way she does, so I am a better person. But vows can be very useful in helping us view the precepts as a serious commitment in our lives. Vows can keep us on the track of making responsible choices, like a double line on a winding country road or even a rein to pull us in when our thoughts are galloping toward hurt-ful actions. So whether one is reading this book in prepara-tion for taking the precepts in a formal way with a qualified teacher, or one is simply considering them more informally, they can be useful in pointing us to the ways in which we get caught in our self-centered thinking.

It is useful to compare the precept vows to wedding vows. Whether in precepts, practice, or in marriage practice, vows are useful for articulating commitments. They act as reminders to return over and over to being awake and taking responsibility for our actions. Just as marriage vows don't guarantee that we won't shoot off some ugly words over a sink full of dirty dishes, precept vows don't guarantee that we won't pocket the spare change from the store clerk's miscalculation. The precepts don't guarantee we won't harm ourselves or others. They are not prescriptions on how to become perfect; they express an aspiration and commitment, as in a marriage, to do our best. Sometimes we express it reluctantly, sometimes painfully, but always with strong intention to see how we hurt others in our insistence that people and events go the way we want them.

A vow is not a forecast of the future. A couple at the altar may have many aspirations about their marriage, but who can tell where it will all go? So too, in taking up the vows of precepts, we really don't know what path they will take us down. We don't know what they might unearth about ourselves, or what deeply held but hurtful beliefs they may challenge or pry loose. In a sense, we are also taking a vow to be willing to face the unknown. So in taking up the way of the precepts, we look to them to help us in facing our blind spots.

Vows simply present our commitment and willingness to persevere. In a marriage, it is one kiss, one meal, one little tiff at a time. Every step, every new day of a relationship is itself the destination and allows the relationship to continue. The vow offers a stick-to-it-ness that helps us be open and honest about whatever conditions life presents to us. Whether we are faced with sticking it out with a difficult partner, with a job that doesn't suit us, with caring for an aging parent, commitment can be the slender thread that allows us to hang in there. And if we hang in there, practicing awareness as best we can, we have the opportunity to learn something very valuable.

Does taking up the way mean we should never have a jealous thought? Never fantasize? Never stretch the truth? Of course not. It just means that we meet these actions as our teachers offering insight into what it really means to be a happy, loving, open individual.

The Dream of Self

> Caught in a dream of self—only suffering.
> Holding to self-centered thoughts—exactly the dream.
> Each moment, life as it is—the only Teacher.
> Being just this moment—compassion's way.
>
> —"Practice Principles" recited at the
> Ordinary Mind Zen School

At the end of each of the meditation sessions at our Zen center, we recite together the above words as a reminder that when we are caught up in our habitual patterns of beliefs and assumptions, we are caught in a dream of self. In other words, the self is none other than our beliefs and assumptions. These words are not meant as a judgment but are offered to us as a reminder that if we live our lives in this way, we're more likely to cause harm to ourselves and others. The way to arouse ourselves from this dream is to hear the wake-up calls in the most ordinary, everyday events. It is in the spirit of this awakening that we take up the way of the precepts.

The Precepts as Teachers of Our Interconnectedness

Buddhist teachings remind us that all life arises out of and continues forth through a vast and fathomless, pure, clear, empty Mind, or Dharma. It is constant, unutterable, unattainable, flawless, selfless, and undifferentiated. And at the same time, this all-pervasive Mind is charged with possibilities.[1] Dharma is the unnamable source of all of life and living—you, me, trees, rivers, rocks, books, bugs, atoms, dreams and wishes, tears and laughter—the entire world of our everyday life. It includes extinction and killing, speech and lies, attainment and stealing, flaws and slander, self-centered anger, differences, and put-downs. But Dharma is even more. It is mutual dependency—nothing comes about on its own. It is what Henry David Thoreau calls "the infinite extent of our relations."

The Net of Indra

There is a metaphor from the ancient Buddhist *Avatamsaka Sutra* that conceives the universe as an enormous net extending infinitely in all directions, protecting and nurturing all of life, nothing excluded. At the juncture of each knot of the net there is a shiny, multifaceted reflective jewel. Because of its many sides, each jewel reflects every other jewel in the net in a vast network of mutual support of each other's existence. It's difficult to imagine the countless number of jewels in a net this size let alone the endless number of reflections on each jewel. No jewel exists without the other jewels. No jewel stands alone. All are interdependent on the presence of others. If one appears, all appear; if one does not appear, none appear. If you were to place one black dot on any one of the jewels, it would appear in all the jewels.

The Net of Indra is a compelling image illustrating unceasing, unobstructed interpenetration and mutual interdependence of all existence. Every action, every word, every thought—our memories, desires, fears, urges, frustrations, happiness, peace, well-being—ripples its effect into the universe. No one, no thing is excluded in this mutual resonance and all-inclusive relationship. As Vietnamese Zen master Thich Nhat Hanh reminds us, we carry in our heart not only our personal joys and sorrows, but also the joys and sorrows that are society itself. When you take action that brings about well-being for yourself, you bring about well-being for the world. When you take action that is harmful to yourself, you bring harm into the world. So Dharma can be thought of as the central law of life—that all of life is one and that all things and events are part of this indivisible wholeness. To follow the teaching of Dharma is to take action that is in harmony with the interrelatedness of all things. Every action has an effect and every effect leads to a cause in an infinite web of life. Zen master Robert Aitken describes this interrelatedness in *The Mind of Clover*:

> You and I come forth as possibilities of essential nature, alone and independent as stars yet reflecting and being reflected by all things. My life and yours are the unfolding realization of total aloneness and total intimacy.[2]

Yet this is not to say that you, me, our neighbor down the street, individuals across the world, do not have some personal individuality. Clearly, individual differences create the multitudinous variations of life. Even though we as human beings share 99 percent of the same genes, the remaining 1 percent is plenty enough for individual differences that are then molded by heredity, culture, society, upbringing, and so forth. So while we are in one sense individuals, at the same time, we are only part of a larger picture, not the whole of it—the self is completely autonomous, yet exists only in resonance with all other *selves*.[3]

The last sentence above reminds us of the paradox of practicing with the precepts. For, while the precepts ask us to watch and question our individual thoughts, words, and actions, we can also learn about ourselves through our resonance with others. The only thing we can know is ourselves, and yet we have to interact with others in order to discover who we think we are.

To Study the Self

The thirteenth-century Zen master Dogen Zenji tells us that the path to freedom and happiness is through coming to study ourselves completely: "To study the self is to forget the self, and to forget the self is to become one with all beings."[4] I take this teaching as a reminder that in order to recognize, indeed experience, my connection with all of life, I must first see beyond the limits of my personal identity. "To forget the self" does not mean that we forget our individual strengths, weaknesses, and preferences. It doesn't mean that vanilla ice cream will no longer be my favorite or that I'll get over my fear of climbing in high places. What it does mean, however, is that I am *this* but not *only this*. Our intention in receiving the precepts is not just to bring awareness to behavior, as one might expect, but to explore, as Dogen Zenji suggests, who we think we are.

THREE

The Dead Spot

The Trapeze

Trapeze artists who seem to effortlessly swing through the air with the greatest of ease win my vote for the most enticing circus performers. They spin out on one bar and midway through, let go, do a twirl or a twist, and seemingly without effort or thought, grab the next bar, which almost miraculously presents itself at their fingertips. They often do their act without a safety net under them to catch a fall. I marvel at their daring and skill at what appear to be effortless swings from one bar to the next. How like our lives. As conditions and events arise we swing into action.

Some years ago, I read an interview with a young performer from a family of trapeze artists. The interviewer suggested that she must be pretty strong physically to be able to control the swings. The young artist answered, "Physical strength isn't really necessary. . . . Sometimes it

For example, if a student is exploring the precept *I take up the way of engaging in sexual intimacy respectfully and with an open heart,* then first she needs to explore what sexual intimacy means to her. Or, if she is working with the precept *I take up the way of taking only what is freely given and giving freely of all that I can,* then she turns to the discovery of what she believes is lacking.

Recognizing the shape and perimeter of our individual identities is not a mysterious study. Simply turning toward investigating our actions in an open, honest way can be our greatest teacher.

can save you if you make a mistake, but if you're relying on strength, you're doing it wrong. The trapeze is all timing. It's letting the trapeze do the work for you." [1]

I would also add to that equation awareness of many conditions. When you think of it, there are so many variables in a swing—the airwaves, the heat, the lights, and the performer's body and concentration on that particular day. A twist one day can be a brilliant move. The next day, it could be a fatal error. It all depends on the conditions present in that moment and conditions change from swing to swing.

The Dead Spot

The trapeze artist went on to say that the most important part of the trapeze action was something called the *dead spot*. The dead spot comes "at the end of the swing . . . when the swinging bar stops moving in one direction and starts moving in the other. Like when you're highest on a playground swing. The whole idea is to use that change of momentum to create the trick." She explained that it is there, in that moment, that the next trick is born.

The reporter noted that swinging on a trapeze is a lot like life—"timing is all." But, as he also observed, "in life it's hard to sit still and wait for the timing to reveal itself . . . life keeps [us] moving and at predictable [or not predictable] intervals, there will be change. The pendulum will literally swing the other way. You can't change that. You can only use it."

I've added a few twists of my own to this act. I like to expand the metaphor to include another aspect of trapeze-swinging—the letting go between bars. I think of the dead spot as that place between swings, when the performer just hangs at point zero before grabbing the next bar. It is the moment of nonaction and not knowing. The events of life offer all types of dead spots.

Our dead spots can take many forms. They can occur at the time of major events, like changing a relationship or profession. It can be the loss of a loved one or indecision over what action to take when faced with a job choice. Whatever it is, no matter how big or small, the dead spot appears when we cannot engage in our habitual way of holding and grasping for the bars, either because we are forced to let go or we willfully launch ourselves into midair. Life pries our fingers loose and no matter how much we try to avoid it, we end up in the suspended moment, not knowing what comes next.

Say you have a medical problem and have to wait several weeks for test results. During that time you may find yourself right in the middle of the dead spot because you don't know what to expect. You might have either a minor problem, which lets you be safe or okay, or a life-threatening illness that could mean your life. For several days you grasp first at one bar and then the next: *I'm going to die* or *I'm going to live*. Our usual reaction to this type of situation is to grasp at whatever relief we can get. How we do this differs according to our systems of defense. For some, it may be assuming the worst scenario. For others it may be only assuming the best. For some it may be clouding awareness.

As I help people explore the precepts, I sometimes wonder what kind of world it would be if we could all just hang for a moment in our own dead spots. We don't have to be trapeze artists to know that dead spot. Sooner or later, if we're lucky, we'll find ourselves awake, suspended between the bars. Of course it's the last place we want to be. But if approached with intelligence, the dead spot can be the key to understanding the reactionary behaviors spinning in the dream of self. We can learn how to work in that split second, when either there is no new bar for us to grasp or our usual favorites no longer work; we have the opportunity to know ourselves in a way that is open to whatever life brings our way.

Just This

When if even for the briefest of moments, we take pause in the dead spot, that moment of nonaction, before we react, we step through the door marked Enter Here and meet life just as it is, in just this moment. It is in this moment of Just This that the trapeze artist finds the most power and creativity. In Just This we meet the power and creativity to break away from our habitual thoughts, emotional matrix, body patterns, and energy that fuel and direct our reactions. So, for example, when someone insults us, with practice we can more quickly turn our awareness to our experience—to thoughts like, Who does she think she is talking to me that way? We can breathe in the presence of the tightening in the shoulders and neck, the heat in the face, the words wanting to form in outrage. Just This is exactly what the words suggest—there is only *this* right now. As one teacher has said, "Wherever you go, there you are." This is the core of our awareness practice—to challenge us to question our assumptions about what makes the world real to us. It turns us toward the realization that any assumption of permanence is exactly that—an assumption. That in truth, Truth can only be expressed as Just This.

As you work your way through the precepts presented in the following chapters, you will learn how to engage in this process and experience Just This for yourself. In time, you may find that you can actually rest for longer periods in the place of no action, between the habitual reactionary swings. In other words, you will be more attentive and at rest in the presence of the worry and anxiety of not knowing, for example, what those medical tests will reveal. Looking and listening to the spinning scenarios of thoughts and the churning sensations in our stomachs, we open ourselves to the full experience of our lives just as it is in this present moment.

The precepts can be a useful tool for helping us learn how to find our way into the dead spot and rest in Just This. For example, when we're out with a couple of friends and someone's name is brought into the conversation for gossip, the beacon light goes on and before we join in, we allow ourselves to experience the moment before the reaction. Maybe we feel a surge of physical sensations as our desire to join in talk rises, especially if the person being discussed is someone for whom we have strong animosity. We continue, breathing, watching, listening.

This moment of nonaction, in which we are completely aware and present in our feelings and bodily sensations, is one in which we are making good, fruitful use of the precepts. When we don't try to escape our experience, the necessity of reaction slowly begins to fade. Instead, we often find that we begin to take actions that best meet the present circumstances or situation. We respond instead of react. We take action that best serves life. What do we do when we find ourselves in the presence of gossip? What do we do when someone just insulted us? What do we do when an emotion within us demands to be numbed? What do we do with any thought or feeling that leads us into reactions that ultimately could be hurtful? Yes, there are short-term strategies that it will often make sense to follow. We can excuse ourselves or change the subject when we're with people who start talking about someone else. We can count to ten or go for a walk before answering the insulting email. These are certainly useful ways to stop our reaction, but real transformation, a dismantling of the reactionary patterns learned deep within our brains and bodies, can only take place by facing the deepest beliefs and fears that drive us toward the next bar. This confrontation can only occur in the dead spot.

Reactions

But what if the trapeze artist, for some reason, doesn't let go and just keeps grabbing for the same bar in the same old way? There are many reasons why she might not take that step into suspension. Maybe the timing is off. Then it would make good sense not to let go. But what if she was too scared to try something new? What if the swinging back and forth on the same bar carried certainty and safety? What if the same old swings are the only swings she knows? She would never experience what our young performer suggests is the most powerful, creative moment of the entire act—the moment pregnant with possibilities.

Again, how like life. As circumstances and events arise in our lives, how do we swing into action? On reflection some of us may find that, like the trapeze artist, we swing on the same old bar back and forth, meeting whatever life brings our way with the same old reactions. For many of us, much of our lives is spent in habitual swings on the same old bar. No matter how unhappy it makes us, no matter how much we know it affects others, it may seem to us the only way to go. The old familiar swings seem safe and to rest for just one brief second in that dead spot can seem daunting. Yet, if we really want to experience the happiness and well-being that comes when we break loose of our habitual reactions of self-defense, then we need to take a much clearer look at our reactive thinking. Lao Tzu points to how we can break these patterns:

> Who can by stillness, little by little
> make what is troubled grow clear?
> Who can by movement, little by little
> make what is still grow quick? [2]

Reactive thinking manifests itself in several ways. Perhaps a boss corrects us for something we did incorrectly and before we know it, we swing into self-defense, rejecting his words. Maybe we gossip about others, pointing out their faults as revenge for some mistreatment. Maybe we distort the truth to cover ourselves. Perhaps we grasp at whatever sensual pleasure excites us or overly depend on approval from others. Or maybe we remain distant and indifferent by isolating ourselves through substances, overworking, tuning out, or turning away from closeness. In the heat of our reactions, we fail to see the reality of a given situation and often end up doing more harm than good. We may have no idea where our reaction stems from, but we continually react in the same way whenever our buttons get pushed. It is the *re* part of *reaction* into which we need to inquire. By observing ourselves through any of the precepts, we are quickly confronted with our reactionary patterns, and how they occur again and again.

Swinging on the same old bars in the same old way without meeting the freshness of the present condition is the difference between reacting and responding to whatever a situation offers us. Struck with the possibility of a life-threatening illness, the first thing, of course, that most of us want is to know the prognosis. But the truth is, we won't have any information until the tests come in. Even then, we don't know what will develop. Being open in this way is often very difficult unless we've cultivated the ability to rest in what is. We often convince ourselves of all sorts of things—even lies.

When we are in that place of not knowing there is no safety net under us. Suspended action. Suspended thinking. Suspended knowing. No stories, no shoulds. Just This— awake and present. It's very difficult to hang there for long, without grasping at whatever gives us a sense of security. But there's a lot to be learned even in just two or three seconds, if we're willing.

Response

The power of resting in the dead spot cannot be overestimated. In time, we don't find ourselves repeatedly swinging from the same bars. Something changes. Something shifts at a very deep level. As new situations arise, we begin to respond instead of react. Our actions are more often responsible actions because they are based on what best meets the reality of the situation. Facing the sink full of dirty dishes, I simply see dishes with a bit of egg and jam. I turn on the hot water, soap the sponge, and begin washing. Dishes are just dishes. Or our boss points out an error, and we say, "Oh, yes, I see what I did wrong. Let me correct it." Or we respond, "I understand that you see that as my error, but I wasn't the person who did it." In either case, we keep the precept of not distorting truth. The key is we've responded in the true sense of the Latin *respondere*—which means *to match*—and are simply matching our responses to the situations that require them.

If we rest in the dead spot, we allow ourselves to recognize the perception of the boss and to include whatever other facts are present in the situation, then we respond. He thinks what he thinks at this moment. He believes it is true that we made an error. We honor his position by really listening and acknowledging what it is he has to say, by resting in the experience of what that brings up for us and then responding. We either agree or disagree. This is quite different from running reactionary thoughts, such as He always thinks I'm making mistakes, or She doesn't appreciate all that I do around this office. Maybe those thoughts are true, but there are options for how we can respond to them. Whatever difficult situations we find ourselves in— in the workplace, with our families, or among friends—can be opportunities to work through reaction into response. This is how we take up the way of the precepts.

FOUR

The Process

I like to think of working with the precepts as a spiraling process that takes us through an exploration of the trapeze swings of our daily encounters. This spiraling process begins by observing our behavior around a specific precept and then circles its way into a deeper understanding of our reactionary patterns and the beliefs that fuel them. Over time we can experience these beliefs as really nothing more than projections of our identity, or the dream of self. As we carry this process into the most ordinary encounters of our lives, we become more aware of deeply held assumptions about the way we and others need to be.

Approaching the precepts in this way nourishes a powerful awareness that can eventually cut through our deepest assumptions and help us live awake and in truth. We can find the freedom to choose an action that takes into account the circumstances present at any given time in any given situation—doing *what best serves life*. Taking action that best serves life means to take action that comes out of being as aware as possible of the many conditions present in any situation. It is action based not on our self-centered view of life but one that considers whatever other conditions our awareness holds in the situation. It includes but is not limited to how the conditions affect us.

When students decide to use the precepts as a focus in their practice, I ask them to begin by focusing on a reaction that they find themselves engaged in. We then begin with that reaction by phrasing it in the form of one of the precepts. For example, one of my students noticed that she often found herself talking negatively about others, sometimes doing it so skillfully that her negative comments were cleverly clothed in seemingly complimentary phrases. So I suggested that she begin with the precept *I take up the way of speaking of others with openness and possibility*. Then we began the first turn of the inquiry—engaging the observer.

Engaging the Observer

The first step in taking up the way of the precepts turns us toward engaging the observer so that we can study the reactionary patterns in our daily life. Just as a good science researcher wouldn't try to stop or interfere with the behavior of the animals under her investigation, so too, at this first stage of working with the precept, we simply observe, using the observational skills developed through our daily meditation practice. So if a student is working with the precept of Not Discussing the Faults of Others, she begins by simply observing herself in action as she speaks of others. The beacon light is on. At this entry step she does not try to stop herself from speaking of others' faults, but rather she gathers data about when and where and under what conditions she gossips.

With patient observation, looking and listening without judging or interfering, our more subtle behaviors reveal themselves to us. As you observe yourself talking about others without trying to change anything, the feelings, thoughts, and bodily sensations that make up the habitual reaction come into clearer focus. For example, you might note that you find yourself often speaking of others through the lens of fault when you're feeling a little uneasy about yourself in some way. The beacon light comes on, perhaps revealing that this way of speaking often arises when you're on the phone or in social situations. After some time practicing in this way, you may find that you talk negatively only about certain people or only with a certain group of people. You may also notice that you find this way of speaking oftentimes kicks in automatically when you discuss others. You begin to see it as a reactionary pattern. With continued practice, you may notice that you get something out of talking about others in this way. You may even have a shadow of a thought that finding fault with others has more to do with something about yourself than about the other person. Perhaps you feel superior or in a stronger, safer position. There are many ways reactionary patterns of behavior can serve our dream of self.

As human beings, we're pretty adept at developing and then relying on habits. Our minds and bodies thrive on frequency, rhythm, and consistency. The problem is that sometimes our minds and bodies lock into taking actions that don't always fit the situation.

Deepening the Observation

Once our habitual swings come into focus, we're ready to deepen our observation by watching, looking, and listening to our bodily sensations, emotions, and thoughts as we engage the precept. It's as if we are zooming in on ourselves with a camera as we swing into a comment like "Jack can never be depended on." How am I standing when I talk to my neighbor about Jack? What's happening to my breath as I speak into the telephone? How am I holding the receiver? Does my hand grip the handset? When that beacon goes on, we encourage ourselves to question: Are there any emotions present? Thoughts? One of my students noticed that when she gossiped about others, she felt puffed up like a bird conserving its heat. She said that she was quite surprised that it made her feel physically taller and bigger. She also noticed a rush of heat in her chest as she began to speak. She actually felt more engaged and noticed a glimmer of an *I am better* thought. This is just one type of sensory reaction that one might notice. Another student reported that he felt as if he had put up a shield of armor around himself. He observed rigidity, anger, and hardness whenever he sensed his self-image threatened.

I suggest that students carry this expanded observation into all their daily activities, from when they get up in the morning to when they go to sleep. The intention is to be awake to actions around a specific precept—on the bus, in the car, at work, wherever and whenever we find ourselves swinging into reaction. Sometimes people report that the observer even switches on in their dreams. You don't need to dream about it, though, for it to have a clear effect on your awareness. One person did the following practice with the precept *I take up the way of meeting others on equal ground.* Every time he found himself in a group of three people or more, he would silently go around, looking at each person and asking himself, How does the self measure itself in relation to this person? He not only would take note of what thoughts arose—I'm smarter, quicker, not as popular, etc.—but also would bring attention to the bodily sensation associated with the thought and any emotions that were present.

Sometimes people begin to question if this way of working doesn't border on self-indulgence. Without engaging the observer, perhaps it would. But used skillfully as a tool to wake us from the self-centered dream, this way of working enhances our ability to identify and dismantle the reactionary patterns of mind and body. Self-awareness is not self-indulgence.

As you begin to do your own exploration of these precepts, you will have the opportunity to work this way in more detail. Don't expect miracles. Don't think that once you decide to work in this way, your reactions and requirements will reveal themselves at your will. For quite some time, you may find that you become aware of your reactions only *after* they've arisen and fallen away. This is quite normal, since our reactions are deeply ingrained patterns by which the brain and body process data. Someone gives you a look in a particular way and before you can even take a breath, the brain has sent out its messages to release certain chemicals, the organs pick it up and spit out the adrenaline, the heart races, the face flushes, and your actions follow the command by issuing forth a verbal threat or an insult.

But there's a great deal of power in awareness. Trust it. The point is that at any moment you can note that you are about to engage or have engaged a precept. That is your point of entry into the practice. Over time, as awareness grows sharper, it will pick up on what's going on deep inside, long before the harsh words hit the tongue or the shrug of defiance reaches the shoulders. This is a journey of the heart and mind. It takes patience to coax our beliefs out of hiding and it takes courage to look into the places we've kept in the dark.

If after a while, you can catch five out of twenty-five times a day in which you react, then you have engaged the beacon of the observer considerably. Don't focus so much on whether the beacon lights up before, during, or after the reaction has taken place. What matters is that you are now taking notice. Just turn your attention to what is right before your eyes in that very moment the light shines forth. At first you will have to engage the beacon purposely and you may feel a little discouraged because you may not see anything about your actions. But keep in mind that it is more natural to be awake than it is to be asleep. It's just that you've become more accustomed to the dream state and have the mistaken belief that you're awake! After some practice you'll begin to notice moments when you're already observing your experience before you even think to do it.

This first step is very important because the very act of stepping aside, even if it is only slightly, to observe our actions is a giant step toward putting those reactions into perspective. It's as if we are standing on the platform to the side of the trapeze and at the same time swinging out. We get to see clearly from a bit of a distance the habitual swings and maneuvers we make over and over as we swing our way through our daily encounters. We may not have a lot of insight into why we do it, but we most definitely see more clearly how we swing.

Requirements

After a student has spent some time observing his reactionary patterns around a precept, I ask him to spiral a little deeper into the inquiry process in order to reveal more deeply held beliefs. These beliefs take the form of requirements that we place upon ourselves and the world. In the above example, my student who was exploring the ways in which he measured himself by others could phrase this as a requirement he has placed on himself: I require myself to be better/less than others and/or I require others to be better/less that me.

At this point, the precept is engaged as a stop sign. The prohibitory aspect of the precept is utilized as another tool by suggesting that we pause to see what comes up. After having practiced self-observation for some time, there is a good sense where and under what conditions this behavior swings into action. Now, when he catches himself about to measure or in the middle of measuring himself to others, he lets the stop sign come up, thus denying himself the reactionary action of measuring himself to others. By stopping in his tracks, he has let go of the trapeze bar and hangs in the place of no action—the dead spot.

Where in the first round of the spiral, the practice was to watch without interfering, now we are trying to stop ourselves before, during, or soon after the reaction. This can be a little difficult at first and is why this step is second. It takes a bit of observing acuity to not just see it, but also to stop it. The energy behind any of the precepts—speaking ill by gossiping about others, taking what's not freely given by pocketing the store clerk's mistake, using substances to cloud awareness, flipping on the TV to space out, misusing sexual energy—is extremely powerful. But because it is more natural for us to be awake than to be in the dream, with patience and persistence, at least part of time, we will wake up before reacting. It needs to be stressed here, however, that the reason we put up the stop sign is not that we are trying to follow some outward moral authority. Rather it is to engage the power of awareness so that we can see more clearly what deeply held beliefs are behind our actions.

Pausing in the moment of no action—the dead spot, as

the trapeze artist says—is the place full of possibilities. Not only can it reveal deeper conditioning, but also it offers a variety of practices to support and help us in resting in the power of just this moment—which is compassion's way. At this point our attentiveness is quick and alert. It's like being at a party or at work and hearing your name mentioned by someone behind you. The head slightly turns so the ear can better hear. The attention is piqued and focused on hearing the words. It is this level of attentiveness we find in the dead spot. Just breathing in and out and keeping the beacon of awareness shining so that sensations, feelings, emotions, and thoughts can become clear.

Sometimes we may deepen the inquiry into the habitual mind/body pattern by posing a simple question like What is this? or What is happening? There may be a quivering in the stomach or a tightening in the jaw. We simply ask, What is this? Keeping in mind that this process is far from linear, in other words, we don't always move from point *A* to point *B*, and so forth, we eventually recognize that our reactions often arise out of beliefs about the way we think we or others need to be. We might call these beliefs *requirements:* I/you should be understanding. I/you should be self-sufficient. I/you should be . . . (you fill in the blank).

How Should It Be? How Is It?

Requirements aren't something we consciously choose. They develop slowly over time from a combination of our unique cultural experiences, our upbringings, and our natural tendencies. Utilizing this kind of probing to reveal the underpinnings of our requirements is not intended as psychotherapy, but rather as skillful means of waking, alerting us to how they fuel our actions. It can reveal the blueprint of the self-centered dream in which we view the world as we think it *should* be rather than how it *is*. Requirements can be likened to colored glasses through which we view all of our experiences. This practice encourages us to, first of all, feel the glasses on our face, and then to try removing them. When we do this, we come face to face with what we are trying to avoid. Requirements relate to our work with precepts because quite often it is when one of our requirements is not being met that we break a precept.

Most people have many requirements. Some are favorites. Some are used only now and again. These requirements can keep us *imprisoned,* bound to swing forever in the same way on the same trapeze. What's it like to live a life in which we expect ourselves and others to always be self-sufficient? And what happens when life comes along and hits us from behind, when those we love go away, we lose our job, or some other condition arises that denies us our requirement? One of my students found that there is a great difference between having the freedom to take actions that enable him or others to be self-sufficient, and actions that stem out of the belief that he and others must *always* be self-sufficient. One action stems from an open, free heart. It truly serves life. This is a response that could relate to the precept *I take up the way of meeting others in the spirit of mutual openness and discovery.* The other stems from the demand of a closed, self-protected heart. It is the reaction that judges and sees others and ourselves from the view of fault. A response that really has engaged the precept is the one that best meets the situation at that time. This is meeting life as it is.

PART TWO

The Precepts

Out of mistakes and obsessions may grow familiarity and relationship.

—John Elder, *Reading the Mountains of Home*[1]

John Elder's words remind me of the true power of the precepts and why I find them so powerful in helping us live our lives with an open heart and a clear mind. As I have stated earlier, the precepts are not to be taken as a yardstick by which we measure our own or others' self-worth. Rather they are gateways through which we can realize the mutual human foibles we all share and the compassion, wisdom, and joy that connect all living beings. It is in this spirit that we take up the way.

FIVE

I Take Up the Way of Speaking Truthfully

When asked, "What is honest speech?" she answered,
"Listen! The brook babbles along the stones."
——from a Dharma talk of mine at the Bay Zen Center

This precept is variously cast as "not lying," "not engaging in false speech," or even, "right speech," but however the precept is stated, it encourages us to consider carefully the very nature of deception, and by doing so, directs us to what is real and true.

Approached with open inquiry into what propels the ways we deceive, *taking up the way of speaking honestly* can help us begin to explore our delusory beliefs and conditioning that prevent us from engaging honestly and wholly in the experience of living. There is an old saying that "a person can't dupe others who hasn't duped himself first." In a world that seems so deeply steeped in all levels and types of deception, sifting through our own forms of deception is not such an easy task. But by turning our awareness toward uncovering the ways in which we delude others, we can come to recognize a deeper betrayal of ourselves and of truth itself. One of my students rephrased this precept in this way:

> *I take up the way of honestly facing the distrust,*
> *uncertainty and fear that propels my tongue to be*
> *disloyal to the truth of this moment.*

I sit at my computer wondering how to begin writing about being truthful. I start and stop, trying to find the right words to talk about truth telling. It's two days before the first day of summer and the window to my office is wide open. I turn my attention from my thoughts about truth and deception toward the sounds around me. I stop and listen. In the kitchen downstairs, the water is running from the faucet as my husband prepares his morning tea. A rooster is crowing in the distance—cock-a-doodle-doo! My neighbor is calling her cat, "Here kitty, kitty." And there it is—honest speech. I've told you, to the best of my perception, how it is. It seems so simple. Speaking truthfully is simply telling it how it is—in that moment.

Try it yourself. Put this book down for a moment. Take a few deep breaths, relax, and just listen. Open your ears to what's happening around you and within your own body. Now simply say aloud what you hear. Pretty simple isn't it? Try it with your other senses. Say what you see as you look out the window, as you run your fingers over the cover of this book, as you taste some water in your mouth. That's it. Sound oversimplified? Only in the scheme of our complicated thinking.

When I looked up the word *deception* in a thesaurus, I found at least twenty synonyms for not speaking truthfully.

Misleading, illusory, and deceiving are just a few, and certainly, deception is not limited to speech alone. We can deceive with looks, gestures, actions. Nevertheless, from the point of view of this precept, which focuses primarily on speech, we can say that not telling the truth can range from a harmless fib like "I'm just on my way out the door," cutting off the telephone solicitor who calls just as we're about to sit down to dinner, to harmful lies to deflect blame and suspicion from our own actions. We can sprinkle part truth with part lie, or we can try to create truth by presenting what we wish were true as if it were fact. Sometimes we lie to prevent others from feeling hurt, like when we lie to a child about something we know will be very painful or when we lie to keep bad news to ourselves so we don't worry loved ones. Sometimes we keep silent and lie by omission, taking the route of indifference. Some of us anguish over the simplest fib while some of us have learned to distrust truth to such an extent that lying has become the habitual way of reacting to events. And there are many variations of deception in between. Finally, deception isn't limited to what we tell others; it also includes what we tell ourselves.

The multifaceted ways of deceiving through speech are what people often first notice in exploring this precept. It is not too difficult to spot an outright lie, like saying something that you clearly know to be false, but there is a grayer zone of falsehoods in which we speak partial truths that include a whole range of deceptive maneuvers. Imagine this. One day you come home exhausted from a hard day at work. A friend calls and asks you to go out to a movie with her because she's feeling a little down. You're tired and really just want to get to bed early. What do you say? Are you honest and tell your friend you're just too tired tonight or are you compelled by something deeper to evade the truth by making up some excuse, like you can't go to the movies because you've got a lot of work to do or you have someone coming over? Or would it be better in this situation for you to drink a cup of coffee, put off your early bedtime until tomorrow night, and go meet your friend? A simple situation such as this one can reveal a great deal of information about the ways in which we do not speak truthfully, even at the expense of our own or others' emotional or physical well-being.

Silence

Silence is a particularly interesting form of deception. Sometimes we keep silence when we should speak. In his 1969 speech "Silence and Speech," Martin Luther King Jr. spoke out against the war in Vietnam and reminded us that "we are responsible not only for the lies we speak, but for the truth we fail to speak."

When fear keeps our tongue still, it's hardly silent. There are plenty of voices screaming loud and clear within us. Perhaps keeping our mouth shut is the best, most skillful action to take, perhaps it isn't. How are we to know? There is no formula. There is no manual for speaking Just This. When I find myself in this type of dilemma, I like to ask myself, Why am I not speaking? What is my intention? How will my words help or worsen this situation?

One of my students, after practicing with this precept for a month, found that she wasn't aware of very many times she failed to speak what was true. She worked in a busy hospital and was often switched between different care units, sometimes told to care for patients with conditions with which she had very little experience. I suggested that she begin by observing her use of words whenever this situation came up. After a week, she found that she wasn't saying much at all and that, indeed, those were the times when she felt most frustrated and angry. So she decided to use this precept as an exploration of silence. When she was asked to do something that in her opinion was not helpful to a patient, she would ask herself, What is my intention in saying something? Given my abilities, what would be in the best interest of this patient, my coworkers, myself? She would then repeat the answer to herself silently, noticing any accompanying thoughts or feelings that would rise while acknowledging to herself what is true.

Sometimes our words ring false because we speak just to fill in the deafening silence. I feel this pressure sometimes when it's time for me to speak to a group, and I'm a bit lost for a subject. But if I'm alert that day, I might remember the words of a Washoe Indian:

> Sometimes the words just don't come, because there is something holding them back. It don't do no good to just make something up. You just can't say it if you don't feel it right. The words don't come. If you just say anything to sound good, you might hurt somebody, or it might come back and hit you hard. You have to sit there and wait for it to come right out of your own body. Maybe it don't come. You can't force it out. You just have to try to live right and then maybe it will come out of you some other time.

The truth of "I don't know what to say" can make us very uneasy and drive us quickly into the dead spot. Many of us aren't used to silence in a world that is filled with explanations and answers, so sometimes our foot ends up in our mouth. But there can be a great deal of honest humility in the silence of not knowing and that dead spot of silence is potent with many possibilities, if we just can rest in that silence for a few moments. Instead of scurrying about here and there looking for answers, it would be good sometimes to pause and question, Who is it or what is that that propels us toward finding all the answers?

The Certainty Principle

An old Buddhist tale tells the story of Mara, the ancient Buddhist god of ignorance, who shows up whenever it seems he can dupe folks into believing what isn't true.

> One day Mara was traveling along the road with some of his attendants and noticed a man doing walking meditation. The man's face glowed with delight. It seems he had just discovered something on the ground in front of him. Noticing the glow lighting the man's face, one of Mara's attendants asked the god what the man has discovered. Mara answered, "It seems he as discovered a piece of truth."
>
> His attendant grew quite excited and exclaimed, "But you are the god of deception, aren't you bothered by the fact that someone has found a piece of truth?"
>
> Mara answered, "I'm not troubled in the least."
>
> "Why not?" asked his attendant.
>
> "Because," Mara replied, chuckling, "No sooner do people discover a little truth than they make a belief out of it."

Someone recently remarked to me that he was quite surprised to find out that the more he explored deception, the more he longed for a clear explanation of the truth. He realized not only did he look for it as a child from his parents, as a student from his teachers, in his profession as a scientist, but also now he realized that he continued his search for the truth in his meditation practice. What's more, he said, he found his own children and his own school students looking to him to provide all the answers. He realized that he and his students were striving for certainty. Certainty is seductive. It makes us feel safe and comfortable. But also, it lulls us into compliance and deadens our inquiry and questioning, lures us deeper into the dream of self. Without it, we might feel like that trapeze artist, hanging between bars. But grasping it, we swing back and forth, ignoring the ever-changing nature of people and events swinging in and out of our lives.

The Buddha said, "Do not believe what I tell you. You must find it out for yourself." I can tell you I hear the sound of a rooster crowing cock-a-doodle-doo in the distant neighbor's yard, but what do you hear and how do you speak what you hear? What is Truth? When asked, "Where is the Great Truth?" the Zen master answered, "It just moved." Truth won't be pinned down. Truth will not be pinned down with the word *the*. How do we pin down the moment? Truth defies definition because it's changing so quickly that as soon as we've tried to grasp it, we've lost it. But it is not only ungraspable; in the words of another Zen master, Truth is also *unutterable, beyond expression.* So, Truth cannot be grasped, written down, or explained in a lecture or a book. This is why it can seem so illusive and distant to us. In a certain sense, then, every time we open our mouth to speak, we have strayed into deception because we have attempted to speak something that cannot be communicated. Yet, communication is inescapable. We do have to speak. Sometimes we even have to speak untruths.

So where does that leave us? If your lover or partner asks if you'll be there for him in the future or if he becomes ill, can you say, "If I really were to speak the truth, I can't say I'll love you in the next moment, let alone if you get sick and need me to take care of you. If I were to be honest with you, I can't even say for certain if I'll feel like sticking around tomorrow morning"? Yet we do have to respond to our partner's question. How do you suppose it would settle with your partner if you just remained silent? Would it be wise to tell a five-year-old, "I really can't say for certain that mommy or daddy will be here to take care of you while you grow up"? When do you lie intentionally? Do you reveal the hiding place of innocent people trying to escape ruthless killers? How do we know when to keep silent and when to speak truthfully?

If we look to the precept as a formula to shape our speech, it will fail us when we are faced with a choice of using words in such a way so that they will best serve life. If we hope our speech meets the reality of the present, we have to face the uncertainty of the future. What was true yesterday may be false today and has no guarantees for tomorrow. Any of the precepts can only serve us to the extent that they can help us face the truth of our actions from moment to moment. The moment of choice—to distort or not to distort—that is where our practice begins.

THE PRACTICE

Begin your practice of this precept by observing the ways in which you do not speak truthfully. Remember to keep the observing stance of the science researcher, paying close attention to when you find yourself distorting truth. You might try by limiting your inquiry to specific situations where you think you may find yourself engaged in deception, but you may also keep it broad. The key is to *listen* to yourself as you speak. I mean *really* listen to the words, the tone of your voice, the pauses and silences, at work, at breakfast with your partner, at the supermarket, in the doctor's office. There is no specific place to do this part of the practice. Just do it. You might be surprised that even if you don't look for ways you deceive, but keep an open ear to deceptive words, voice inflection, and body language, you might still find quite a bit. Remember, the invitation goes out only to the observer, not the judge. And if she does show up anyway, then we just put her in her place, nodding *Hello judge,* then turn the attention toward observing the sound of the voice, the sensations of the body.

In the example earlier in which my student watched the ways in which she handled her work in the hospital, she noticed that indeed she wasn't always just silent. In fact, she often did speak, responding to her supervisor with the compliant words, "That's fine." As she really began to listen, she heard those two little words—*that's fine*—in many situations, not just at work. She uncovered a reactionary way of expressing compliance.

She also realized that she often didn't become aware that she hadn't spoken truthfully until long after the incident had passed. Don't be surprised if this happens. At whatever point in time you wake up to the fact you've not spoken truthfully, that moment is your point of entry into the precept. The event can be as recent as three seconds ago or as long ago as several days. In this early stage, you're just trying to discover the reactionary patterns—under what conditions distortion takes place, so as a point of reflection, it doesn't matter if the beacon light goes on before, during, or after you have distorted the truth. For example, my student began noticing that not only did she not speak up at work, but also she often went into silence when she had a disagreement with her partner or one of her kids. The beacon of light was revealing a much wider reactionary range.

Once you've identified a few typical situations, you're ready to inquire a little deeper. Now, at whatever point you realize you've engaged in a deception, turn your awareness inward and feel your body. Are there any sensations like heart pounding, dry mouth, blushing, or a sinking feeling? See if that sensation wants to name itself as guilt, shame, fear, or whatever. Don't demand an answer. Just invite it. Notice what sorts of thoughts are present and notice if they string together in a story line. What is that story? *I'm bad. I'll never get this. I'm found out. What will they think? How can I cover this?* Are you thinking of further deceptions to cover the last deception? The mind might be racing pretty fast at this point. It's not necessary to catch all the thoughts. Just one. Then just repeat it to yourself: "Having a thought that . . ." You've just spoken truthfully! Don't try to change anything. The purpose is to simply bring the attention to what you're experiencing and be honestly in its presence.

If you do this for some time, over quite a few occasions, you'll begin to notice that the lens of your awareness grows stronger and quicker. It's as if we begin to move backward on the line so that the beacon or stoplight goes on a lot quicker as you engage in a deception. One of my students reported that he felt he hardly ever communicated without deceiving in some way. People often report that they think they're engaging more often in the reaction, when in fact, they are just waking up to how often they do it. This can be a difficult time when our self-judging guilt mind takes over. But we handle the judging mind as we do any other thought/emotion/body reaction. Label. Feel. Breathe and move on.

It is at this point that it is useful to engage the precept as a stop sign that says "Stop before you proceed." Just to stop the action is not enough, however. Saying to yourself, "I'm not going to speak deception in this situation" is useful to a certain extent, of course, but leaving it there will not drive you into a deeper understanding of the falseness of your beliefs. So stop the action, but then begin the inquiry. The stop brings us to the dead spot so that we can fully experience the moment of Just This.

Awareness deepens within the pause. You are between the bars on the trapeze, just before speaking (or not speaking). You are in the dead spot. It is right here that the deception is unveiled by delving further into the experience. It is important to keep in mind the spirit of the Zen riddle here. You are not demanding an answer, but rather suspending in open inquiry into the question: What's the worst thing that could happen if I spoke the truth here? The question is put forth but then released. It's as if you send out a probe into the darkness and simply are open to what eventually is revealed. The real power is in the questioning, not in the answering.

Eventually—and there is no timetable or set number of times we need to go through this—when you are ready, an insight will begin to emerge. You will not only know it in the gut; you will feel it and breathe it in its complete presence. My student who is the nurse worked with this precept for several months before she began to have a sense that what she was trying to keep silent was the belief that if she said what was on her mind, then she would be rejected. She allowed herself to experience the rising and falling experience of rejection whenever it came up by feeling it in her body, opening for as long as she could to it. At first, just a moment or two, and over time, longer and longer periods of time—pounding heart, closed chest, just breathing in and out. Over and over, she paused in open stillness, allowing the sensation labeled *rejection* to rise and fall away—moving, changing, constant flux.

In the beginning you may only be able to be in this dead spot for a fraction of a second. But over time, you will find it easier. It's much like when you are getting ready to go into the water at a lake or ocean and you first put your big toe in the freezing water, thinking you'll never get your whole body in. If you stick with it though, much to your surprise, little by little you find yourself swimming and encouraging your friends to jump in—"the water's just fine!" My teacher, Charlotte Jōko Beck, often refers to it as "the eye of the storm." At the very center of a storm lies stillness and peace.

What we experience by hanging in the dead spot is the groundlessness of our belief that we must be untruthful to our experience. It is the truthfulness of Just This. What we think of as an unbearable experience, one that must be avoided by engaging in silence or falsehoods, is really not much more than energy manifesting in a certain way in our body and thoughts. We come to know intimately the many subtle ways we intentionally deceive in an attempt to escape deeply held assumptions about our identity—our *dream of self*. When we can experience for ourselves the transitory nature of the belief, then it no longer has us in a strong hold. We are a little freer from our requirements—freer to speak truthfully.

CONVERSATIONS

Student: What is the difference between helping others because I want to or because it needs to be done and helping others because I'm deceiving myself? How can I know the difference?

Diane: It depends on the situation. Our choice of action always depends on our ability to see the conditions clearly. In fact, this is the whole point behind all the precepts—to take the best action given all the circumstances. So we might say, "No; I can't do that. I don't have time." Or, if it's something that must be done, regardless of how tired we are, we can perhaps ask for help, or just do it, without the story line.

Student: I'm still not clear how to know when it's okay to not speak truthfully. For example, when it would be best to keep my mouth shut or to lie.

Diane: Always, always, always, it comes back to the question, What is my intention? For that matter, in any of our actions, not just speech, we always look to this question. But to know our intention, first we need to find our hiding places. So that's why we begin this work by first being honest with ourselves about what we're up to. Only then do we have a chance to meet each moment of life with openness and honesty. When we can do that, even for a millisecond, then we don't find Truth, we *are* Truth—genuine, open, naked—wholly and fully.

SIX

I Take Up the Way of Speaking of Others with Openness and Possibility

> At every meeting we are meeting a stranger.
> —T. S. Eliot, *The Cocktail Party*[1]

T. S. Eliot's words resonate in my mind as I catch myself dropping a comment to my husband about someone we both think is *not very reliable*. I question, How do I know what this person's been up to since we last met? Why do I choose to freeze his image in my mind by faulting him as *unreliable?* What have I hung onto in the interval since our last meeting? These are some of the questions we take up when working with the precept *I take up the way of speaking of others with openness and possibility*. Often worded as Not Discussing the Faults of Others, this precept invites us to question deeply the assumptions and beliefs that find their way into our comments as we speak disparagingly of others. One of my students words it this way:

*When I talk about others, who is speaking? Fear and
shame inside push critical words outside. I vow to
pause so the distress in the mind and body can speak.*

Choose a scenario. You're angry and hurt after an argument with your partner, a friend, or a relative, and so you
pick up the phone (or jot off an e-mail) to someone else,
telling them all about this person's faults, blaming him or
her for the argument. Or maybe you're out with a group of
friends and what starts as an innocent discussion becomes
a vehicle for gossiping negatively about mutual acquain-
tances. Perhaps you've just read about the latest exploit of
your favorite *demon* public figure, and so you find yourself
bad-mouthing the politicians. These are only a few possibilities describing the types of situations in which we might
find ourselves talking about another's faults.

Some social psychologists call this human tendency to
fault others "in-group/out-group behavior." This social
theory describes an individual's hope to solidify her bonds
with an in-group by speaking disparagingly about people
not in that group. Although I am certainly not claiming
that this theory accounts for all instances of finding fault
with others, I think it can be useful in exploring the cost
of such a common behavior. As one social psychologist
states, although "categorizing people as in-group or out-
group members may help individuals create a positive social identity and thus feel good about themselves . . . it is a
fundamental cause of prejudice."[2] When we speak disparagingly about others, what do we get out of it? How
does it serve our self-centered dream?

Standing alone in a disagreement or a disappointment
is not always easy. Sometimes we turn to others not to
hurt another person but to make ourselves feel supported.
Maybe our need to have other people see things as we do

reveals our own discomfort in what we feel ourselves. But we can also realize that speaking of another person's faults to someone may be a strategy to get others to share our criticisms of people, reminding us of our human tendency to create in-groups. It's not really that difficult to get someone to share in our faultfinding of others, but if we're really to learn what fuels our actions, then we have to stand alone in our questioning. When we choose to not speak disparagingly of others, this is the choice we make.

We learn this behavior pretty early in life. Children figure out as early as preschool that they can get buddies by sharing secrets and talking about a playmate.

Newspapers sell papers, talk shows get listeners, and the gossip columnists flourish as they feed what seems an insatiable appetite for being the character judge of others. Not only does gossip and faultfinding make the self feel better, it also sells! Look at the current popular TV shows that put people together in such a way that they are forced to indulge this deeply rooted human tendency to speak ill of others. But it's not just in these explosive, competitive dynamics that we pick at each others' weaknesses for personal gain. Gossip, for most of us, is part of everyday life.

When another person's name comes up, how do you engage in that conversation and not fall into the old pattern? Between sharing information and discussing faults lies a universe of self-centered thinking. This precept doesn't mean that we don't acknowledge a person's weaknesses or strengths (or even give them praise), but it helps us know the difference between acknowledging something as information—something someone does—and assuming that they *are* what they do. So, if you're being asked if you think Joe would be a good person to work on a project that requires some math ability, you just pass on some information about the fact that math isn't his strong point. You don't have any personal investment in your statement.

Personal investment is a way to think about the intention of our words. This is what really matters. We can respond to an inquiry with openness, shade the information with a bit of a judgment, or leave out all the information and present not a fact but a criticism of that person. We may think that we are being direct and honest, but if we are unaware of our intention, even in communicating a simple fact, a subtle voice inflection can turn a communication of that fact into a subtle put-down. It may be very important to communicate the fact that a person's actions have been harmful to others. It is another thing, however, to freeze our view of that person by speaking of him as if that is his permanent way of being.

The Conversation Within

Even though I have been talking about freezing others from the point of view of speech, I think this precept points as well to the unspoken faultfinding conversations we have within in our thoughts. So, in a broader view, this precept invites us to not only speak of but also *meet* others with openness and possibility. It is true that speaking disparagingly aloud about another person can have far-reaching effects, but at a deeper level, the mind that is seized by a frozen view of another, even if the thoughts are unspoken, is not capable of being open and awake. It has been my experience that some of our most deeply entrenched faultfinding is for those with whom we have the closest relationships, especially the critical views children hold of their parents and parents have of their children. I am not speaking here of those criticisms we may pass through as children and teenagers, but the frozen perceptions we hang onto. One of my students who was working with this precept shared the following insights:

> Whenever my Dad's name came up, I didn't have anything good to say about him. I had him pegged as just plain hardheaded and stubborn. I thought I knew him, and I held onto my ideas about who I thought he was. Now that he's growing older and his memory isn't so good, he needs me to help him out a little; I'm forced to spend some time with him. I just can't use the excuse that he is impossible to be around. So I'm doing something like you described you did with your mother. I schedule short visits with him where I just hang out with him for short periods of time, trying not to expect anything. It isn't easy, but I'm beginning to sense something else behind his toughness. Practicing with this precept in this situation really has clarified how much I want to hold onto my glass picture of him. But there are moments, right before I react to the judgment I feel in his words, when I can just listen to those words, even when his stories repeat themselves. I've heard them before, but now I really hear them as his experience of life— tough, hard, and hostile. And as I begin to sense his tightness and rigidity as a defense, I'm also noticing some of that same rigidity and toughness in myself. I thought I had him figured out but all I really had was a frozen view of him. I've hung on to my criticism of him as a way to propel me away from him and solidify the defenses around my own pain.

What is most striking about this person's insight is how his willingness to rest in the dead spot, just listening openly to his father's message, opened a door through which he could enter into his own deeply held beliefs. He realized that it was his choice whether to keep swinging from one reaction to another or to stop, look, listen, and respond to his experiences.

Avoiding Ourselves

Another one of my students who was working with this precept had the following experience. His sister had called him on the phone, as she had done many times before, asking for money. He hung up the phone and found himself complaining to his wife about how his sister "is such an irresponsible screw-up." Not long after, however, the precept sign above the door lit up, reading Enter Here. He realized that his words were spoken as a reaction, and he had just frozen his sister in a negative way. He asked himself the very simple but powerful question: How do I think she should be? And answering honestly—that is, how he was *really* thinking—he responded, She shouldn't ask me for money. Then he asked the second part of the question: How is she? There could only be one truthful answer, one that simply states the situation as it is—She is asking me for money. How do I think it should be? How is it? These are clear beacons of light that will always keep us on course. The *should be*'s of our thinking are our requirements. He then turned his attention toward his body, noting that his breathing was short and that his jaw was clenched—another signal that he was in reactionary mode. Again, he asked himself, How do I think she should be? His answer revealed a deeper level of the requirement: She should always take care of herself and be self-sufficient.

After identifying the requirement behind his reaction to his sister, my student continued his practice by exploring the ways he might have similar requirements for other people. He watched and listened in his daily encounters as he engaged the requirement that people should always take care of themselves, noting how he reacted when they did not.

Whenever this situation came up he would turn his attention toward his body and the thoughts that arose. After working this way for several months, he found that often, when he was viewing others from the perspective of faults, underlying that reaction was the belief that people should be perfect. Once more, he found that he often included himself in that judgment. So when he needed to ask for help, he noticed that he often felt uncomfortable. He found to his surprise that the way he valued most people and the extent to which he was open to them was the degree to which they matched his requirement that people should always take care of themselves—be self-sufficient. And he realized that this requirement was not just for his sister, as he had originally perceived. Instead, by using his initial reaction to her request for money as a point of entry into the precept, he found that he believed that he and everyone else *should* always be able to take care of themselves—to be self-sufficient.

Such beliefs are what we hold onto dearly because they make us feel safe and in control. So, when life meets our requirements, we may feel comfortable, but when life does not meet our requirements we swing into reaction.

What's the Worst Thing That Could Happen?

Then my student took another turn in the spiral of inquiry by asking the question: What's the worst thing that could happen if she didn't take care of herself? Asking this question is a useful tool as part of any inquiry. Keeping the awareness open, he noticed a shift in his bodily sensation as a quivering feeling dropped into his belly. He put out a gentle probe by asking the question without looking for an answer. He just rested in the openness of the quivering in his belly. Then out of his experience bubbled up the word *sad*. In another turn in the spiral, he rested in this dead spot. He remained with the full sensation that was labeling itself as *sad,* allowing the full range of the experience. As he opened more to the awareness of sadness, he felt a twinge of fear. Breathing, opening, sitting in the stillness of the dead spot, he began to realize that it was not just *his* sadness and fear that he was touching, but also his sister's sadness and fear, and perhaps the sadness and fear of all those people who have come to be in the position of not being able to take care of themselves—the homeless young man he passed on the street the day before, the orphans begging for food in a third world country, the helpless looks on the faces of starving people that appear on magazine covers and television news. He began to understand that it was this pervasive sadness and fear that he was trying to avoid. It wasn't just about him, and it wasn't about his sister's faults. This understanding came from just one moment of an open heart.

Meeting the Stranger

When we meet others as strangers, our hearts are open to possibility, change, and reconciliation. We haven't decided what one another is, and only know that person as she presents herself in this very moment. Yesterday, you may have exchanged a few harsh words and thought her disagreeable, but today, in this moment, where is *disagreeable?* I like to think of our faultfinding as tinted glasses obscuring a clear view of who or what we meet at any given time. If you meet that person with the words of yesterday echoing in your mind, then your glasses are tinted *disagreeable.* You cannot meet the other as the stranger. How do we assume or not assume that a person has changed since yesterday? As long as we insist on seeing him through our memories, those glasses will not allow us to meet him openly and with possibility.

But to meet others as strangers, we have to enter the gap of not knowing, the dead spot, because we hang in suspended judgment as we face the other person. If we have this person figured out, then we don't have to experience what it might feel like to be in the gap not knowing. And when we gossip, we assure ourselves that we don't have to be alone in what we feel. This is the paradox of this precept; in order to truly know someone, we have to be open to the possibility of change, and admit that we can only truly know that person in the present moment.

The Way It's Made

Studying the ways in which we discuss the faults of others can reveal much about the ways in which we place walls between ourselves and the world in general. When even the more subtle self-serving intentions are added onto the words we convey about other people, we distance ourselves both from them and ourselves. By creating this separation, we encourage the specialness of me. Feelings of inadequacy, imperfection, fear, and shame may be temporarily assuaged, but they are only pushed aside to reappear at another time. We deeply harm them when we speak of others in degrading ways, and we harm ourselves as well because we deny acceptance, compassion, and generosity as part of the fullness of life. As James Baldwin says:

> It is a terrible, an inexorable law that one cannot deny the humanity of another without diminishing one's own; in the face of one's victim, one sees oneself.[3]

My father-in-law had a wonderful Italian phrase he used when others would, in a disparaging way, point out another person's weaknesses. He would say, "*È fatto cosi!*"—"That's the way it's made." How complicated everything becomes when we forget this very simple truth—we are as we are, however we got made this way. His statement doesn't deny the truth about the person, but at the same time, it accepts them as they are without putting them down. But this is never enough for most of us. We rarely accept ourselves as we are, let alone our children, parents, friends, partners, coworkers, teachers, and so forth. And the sadness is that until we can be open to ourselves fully, we can never hope to view others as they are. We will always see them as less than or more than. This is the true meaning of *fault*. From the Middle English *faulte,* meaning lack, and the Latin *falsus,* we have come to the modern English meaning of *fault* —imperfection. The imperfection we see in others is born out of the thought of *lacking* and *untrue*. When we blame, gossip, speak disparagingly of others, that action stems from the belief that we ourselves are less than something. What if we were to investigate this *less than* in our all our actions, all our thoughts, all our speech? What if we were to allow ourselves, even for a moment, to rest in the sensory experience of *less than,* feeling it vibrate as energy within the body? Watching, observing as the mind and body vibrate *less than*. We may suddenly find ourselves at point zero:

not more than, not less than. In this moment, there is no need to be more than or less than. There are no faults. It's just "as it's made." The words of the Zen ancestor Bodhidharma resonate in my ear: "In the realm of the flawless Dharma, not expounding upon error is called the Precept of Not Speaking of Faults of Others."

THE PRACTICE

A good way to explore this precept and how to use it for everyday decision making is to try out the following exercises for a week or two. Remember, there is no timetable and no race to be won. You may find that you only get to point one. That's fine. Once you bring up the intention to explore your reactions in this way, the observer is activated and over time will become stronger.

Stop. Take inventory. Take one week to begin noticing the obvious and subtle ways in which you talk about others—overtly, surreptitiously, covertly. Keep a journal.

Look. Focus in. Choose one or two specific ways in which you talk about others and where and under what conditions you do it.

Listen. Hear your words as you speak in these particular situations. Pay close attention to the tone of your voice, noticing what happens to your voice and to your word choice when you stop simply sharing information and begin discussing faults. For example, "Harry can't be depended on. He doesn't carry through with tasks." This may be factual information; is your tone implying fact or is it finger-pointing? Is the voice snide or sarcastic? Or is it neutral, just relaying a fact?

Experience. Notice if there seems to be any emotional charge present. You might notice it makes you feel good to talk about someone else. Maybe it relieves some bodily tension by letting out some steam. Sometimes people say that they feel physically bigger, stronger. Your body sensations are a good indicator here. If you're feeling some tightness or other discomfort, there's a good chance that your comments are fueled by some negative feelings. Continue looking, listening, and experiencing in this way until you clarify the emotion. For example, you might notice there is really some jealousy fueling your comment.

Repeat. Say again the sentence about Harry, changing it to, "It's been my experience that Harry doesn't always carry through on tasks." Notice the difference that is conveyed. In the first sentence, you are freezing your perception of Harry into a static entity. This is a perception that can only be false. In the second sentence, you are just communicating behavior you have witnessed with Harry. One closes off to the continual opening and creation of a *Harry.* The other allows him to be as he is. And of course what we close off is not just Harry, but our openness to much more. Speaking of the faults of others is harmful not just to the other person, but also to ourselves.

Respond. It is what you do with this new statement about your experience that's important. Just because Harry hasn't followed through on tasks in the past, do you stop giving him tasks altogether? Or do you keep giving them to him with the knowledge that he is capable of change, and if given the opportunity, he could follow through? Another Zen teacher reminds us, "A so-called fault is a weak place where character can change."[4] If we don't invest ourselves in allowing a weakness to strengthen, then we have not fully experienced the practice of this precept.

I'm reminded of Mr. Daly's response to my year of deceiving him about my paralegal skills. Instead of berating me or outright firing me, he responded by finding a way to help me. I believe that what he saw in my deception was what some people call *chutzpah* and that, if channeled correctly, could help me overcome many of the obstacles I would have ahead of me. If he had frozen his perception of me as a person who lies, then I may not have had the opportunity to move past that perception. I did not realize all this then, but I would hope that perhaps even a few of the hundreds of students I have met as strangers through the last thirty years of teaching will have benefited by Mr. Daly's willingness to meet me with openness and possibility.

Deepening the Inquiry

What Am I Adding?

Once we've really engaged this precept, we have the opportunity to more deeply explore the driving power behind our speech. Ask yourself: What am I adding on to the information I am conveying? Again, be sure to listen carefully to your tone and words. For example, if you hear someone yell at his friend, you could say to yourself, that man is mean. But if you allow yourself to simply rest in Just This, you would say to yourself, that man is yelling at his friend. By simply stating the man's behavior, you haven't found fault, nor have you frozen *what* he *is*. This precept helps us reveal what we add to facts, perhaps mixing a bit of the truth with fiction.

Finding fault with others also extends to larger situations. We find fault with the government, the schools, and the *establishment*. Every day we're presented with trivial and not so trivial information about the world through the media, other people, and our own perceptions. How are we to sift out the true from the untrue? How does this relate to blame, and what do we get out of blaming? It's easy to point fingers at what's wrong in the world. Even though it may be a fact that many of our leaders' actions are not in the best interest of the world's population, who are we serving when we blame? By blaming we relieve ourselves of the responsibility of taking action ourselves, believing it's someone else's responsibility, someone else's *fault.* Again, it seems that our blame and negative speech seem to say more about ourselves than others. Think about the following process of investigating what speaking disparagingly can tell you about yourself.

1. Ask yourself, What does talking about this person in this way do for my own self-image? For example, do you feel better about yourself in some way when you fault someone else? Ask, How does speaking of this person's behavior as faults serve me? Why do I really do it? Does it justify your own behavior? Do you feel more accepted by the people you're with? Does it make you feel important? In other words, you may find that by saying another has faults, you feel you're not alone in your own perceived faults, or it makes you feel better—I'm bad, but *he's* worse. Either way, our speech can be a way to avoid the deep belief of being *less than.*

2. Now try seeing yourself in the other person, and honestly try to find examples in yourself when you have been like the person you are discussing. Change the statement from "Harry is undependable" to "How am I undependable?" Watch for situations in which you may not follow through. In other words, look at your own behavior. The idea is to keep an open awareness about your behavior without judgment or even trying to change it, although that may happen quite naturally once you become aware of your actions. What is your experience now? How do you feel about this other person? About yourself? Perhaps

77

you feel less judgmental of her, or perhaps you notice some guilt or some other feelings arise.

3. Now bring yourself into the dead spot by exercising the prohibitory aspect of the precept. Stop yourself from speaking disparagingly about Harry. Ask yourself if, right in this moment, I do not find fault with Harry, what's the worst thing that could happen? Stay open. If any feelings, emotions, or bodily sensations arise, label them and rest with them, breathing in and out. Allow yourself to enter into Just This. This particular question brings us to the core of our behavior and if we stick it out, we can find what fuels it. In other words, what we get of speaking ill of others. If you're in a group, make an attempt to stop yourself from talking about others by removing yourself from the group or biting your tongue. Stay open to your reactions as above.

4. Now consider, What would your relationship to this person be if you simply acknowledged her behavior without finding fault with it?

CONVERSATIONS

Student: What about when we keep silent about a person when we know something negative about them? I don't mean like in lying, as we talked about in the speaking truthfully precept. But say, for example, that I'm with a group of people and someone makes a comment about how wonderful a person is, but I know this person has acted unethically. It could be someone we all know, even a spiritual teacher. If I keep silent, is this a statement of sorts?

Diane: This reminds me of instructions many of us may have heard as children, "If you can't say something good about a person, don't say anything." My own feeling is that we can't get off the hook so easily if we truly want to engage in what's going on. The question is what is our intent in keeping silent? Sometimes silence would be the best course of action. If there's a lot being said, and you can't add any useful information, you may choose to remain silent. But sometimes silence is louder than words. Nothing spoken with good timing can speak volumes. On the other hand, history reminds us of the havoc and human suffering that can come out of people remaining silent.

Student: What about the opposite of seeing others from the point of view of fault? I find that sometimes I will only praise certain people. Isn't this another way of freezing my perception of them?

Diane: Yes, a trickier version, but nevertheless this is the same thing. Remember, the practice is to reveal how we use faultfinding to solidify the self's identity.

Student: I'm wondering about your comments about the difference between speaking and thinking about another person's faults. Are you suggesting that thinking about another's faults is just as harmful as actually speaking the thought?"

Diane: It's been my experience that if we can catch the thought, then we're more likely able to do some of the practice with it. So, in that sense, there is a huge difference between thought and action. But as I mentioned earlier, the thought finds its way to the tongue with lightning speed, and there's all kinds of juicy stuff in between. Most of the time, we're not awake to what we're doing until we hear the words escape our lips, or we get hit with the repercussions of our words.

SEVEN

I Take Up the Way of Meeting Others on Equal Ground

> To be humble is not to make comparisons. Secure in its reality, the self is neither better nor worse, bigger nor smaller, than anything else in the universe. It is nothing, yet at the same time one with everything.
>
> —Dag Hammarksjöld, *Markings* [1]

This precept shines the beacon light on the overt and subtle ways we use others as a yardstick to measure our self-worth by placing ourselves above or below others. It is sometimes worded Not Praising Self at the Expense of Others, or Not Praising Yourself While Abusing Others. The previous precept explored the ways we demean others and ourselves by viewing them from the perspective of faults. In this precept we explore what prevents us from meeting others on equal ground. I do not mean equal talents, abilities, strengths, or weaknesses. Rather I mean equal as human beings. This precept reveals the realm of competition, and how we often view life as a game of winners and losers. Another of my students has phrased it this way:

> *Do I exist outside the realm of judgment and comparison with others? Do others exist when I spin in the realm of fantasy and belief? Insecurity, anger, and shame bar the way. I vow to let frozen breath, pounding heart, and churning stomach lead me through.*

There are many overt and subtle ways we avoid feelings of unease with ourselves by measuring ourselves against others. Most commonly recognized are the ways in which we put ourselves above others while putting them down. This attitude assumes a superior, more powerful stance. It places us in the realm of competition and one-upmanship. Measuring ourselves to others is not just limited to speech, however. It also includes the actions we take with people. For example, we avoid, ignore, or exclude others in our activities. We put ourselves above others not only as individuals but also as groups; no matter what side of an issue they are on, we may claim a superior, enlightened view. When we speak or act in this way, clarity, discovery, and true dialogue are lost.

During the Vietnam war, the Vietnamese Zen teacher Thich Nhat Hanh spoke before a liberal, politically active audience in Berkeley, California. When asked about taking political action, he told the audience that taking action was important, but more important was to try remember that they are not helping bring peace as long as they place themselves in a morally superior position. He reminded us that we can be very good at writing letters but very poor at opening our hearts and minds to those who oppose us.

As individuals we can also measure ourselves to see where we stand as lovers, parents, friends, coworkers, even Zen students. Examples of how we use this strategy subtly or overtly to avoid deeper feelings such as unworthiness, vulnerability, and fear are all around us.

Even though we may not consciously place ourselves above others as a way of measuring our self-worth, we can know if we're in the game of competition by watching our reactions when we make a mistake. Say, for example, you forget an important appointment. Do you quickly justify your actions by finding excuses? Do you blame or find fault with something else? The point is, when we jump to our own defense, we place ourselves above the situation. What is at risk if we say, "I'm sorry, I forgot the appointment"? This is more than simply speaking truthfully, it's also being humble—*neither better not worse.* We forgot the appointment. That's it. What do we add on to it? What is the voice that automatically jumps in defense? When we can acknowledge our fallibility, we know true humility and instead of reacting, respond by saying "I am sorry."

When our attention is focused on maintaining ourselves above others, then in actuality, a closing off and separation occur. Opportunities to realize our connection are sacrificed. We place all our energy into covering our weaknesses and mistakes. Working with this precept not only can help us see the ways we judge others, but also, in that process, can help us face more openly and compassionately our own mistakes.

An indigenous tribe in Tasmania has an interesting community ritual. When something happens in which someone behaves unskillfully, thus upsetting the balance of the community, the group comes together around the fire to reenact the situation. For example, if a man yells at his wife a lot and chases her out of the hut, causing havoc in the village, he is brought before the community, not to be judged or reprimanded, but rather to help him see the absurdity of his behavior. Members of the tribe role-play the scene between him and his wife in a lighthearted way. The villagers, including children, all take part, laughing, joking, and mimicking the absurdity of the behavior until the man himself relaxes and also realizes the absurdity of his actions. Interestingly enough, even his wife takes part in the villagers' dramatization. Before too long, the whole scene turns into a big party and the husband and wife provide food for the rest of the villagers. The purpose of the ritual is to acknowledge their fallibility openly so that they can put it into perspective, even laugh at it. This is an uncommon but very sensible way of dealing with our behavior. Instead, many of us either measure ourselves as *less than* or *better than* others, often taking action that has hurtful consequences that can reach far into the future.

The requirement to place ourselves above others is often fueled by the stories we believe about ourselves in relation to others. For example, you go into work one day and notice that your coworker is busy at his desk and doesn't look up to greet you. If your thought is, He's just busy and didn't notice me, then that's fine. But what if your thought is, He's ignoring me; he doesn't like me? Sometimes this type of thought can fire off a put-down of the person at the first opportunity, tying into a thought like, I'm not important enough. How is this situation putting yourself above others? If we look a little more deeply, however, there might be something there. When we put ourselves above others, we separate in some way. Can I be sure that my coworker is ignoring me, let alone that I'm not worthy? What's the truth of the circumstances in this situation? It may be that he doesn't even hear me come in, or that he's engrossed in his work.

Sometimes, placing ourselves above others can take the form of being the harder worker, the more responsible person. Here's an example. You and your partner come home from work and are very tired. The kids are hungry and it's time to cook dinner. You know your partner is tired and he or she knows you're tired. So who's going to get dinner on the table? Your partner collapses on the couch and says to you, "You'll have to cook." There are two ways you might head for the kitchen. One is with the thought, I'm tired, but one of has to do it, and I guess it's me. Another strategy would be to turn this situation into a way to elevate yourself. How do you suppose that process might go?

CONVERSATIONS

Student: In this kind of situation, maybe I'd have the thought, "When I'm really tired in the future, she better do it for me."

Diane: Okay. First thought. What might come next?

Student: Maybe the thought, "What a good person I am."

Another Student: For me, in that situation, I might note resentment or martyrdom.

Diane: "How good I am! What a good and suffering person I am." Now there's a very long measuring stick! Where does that thought put your partner? In other words, if I'm the good person, then what does she have to be?

Student: Less than good.

Diane: Less than good. Yes. As soon as we enter into a comparison, we have entered into a judgment that separates and places me above the other. So if I'm good, then she must be less than good. If I'm a martyr, then she's got to be someone who needs to be saved. What about the resentment? The *why me,* Why do I have to be put into this situation? pattern of thinking. Well, guess who chose to cook the dinner? You did. But why the resentment? What's that about?

Student: I think when I feel resentment, I haven't really given over to just doing what needs to be done. I do it, but there's a sense of holding back.

Diane: Yes. The hands move without the heart. The hands are really measuring.

Student: And if I'm not being recognized as good, the anger and resentment come in.

Diane: And what if you just cooked dinner because that action would best serve life in this particular set of circumstances?

Student: Then my heart would move my hands.

Diane: Without question.

Measuring Up

Measuring ourselves in terms of how much we do for others can be tricky. A good signal that we're acting out of a requirement, however, can be if we note some upset if we are not acknowledged for our actions. When you don't get appreciation, how to do you react? Do you have thoughts like, Look at all I've done and no one's patting me on the back or telling me what a great job I did? Do you get angry or feel rejected and unappreciated? Of course, in a certain sense, we all like to be acknowledged when we do things for others. I am not suggesting that there's anything wrong with this, but if we are doing for others in order to measure our self-worth in some way, or to measure up to someone else's expectations, then I would say that our helping comes with a price tag.

You can work your fingers to the bone; you can be the most capable person on the job; you can be an understanding partner and a caring parent, but as long as you look for confirmation of self-worth through helping others, then there's something to look at there.

Not only do we place ourselves above others, but also we can place ourselves below others. This is a particularly covert form of behavior and is worth exploration. If you find that you habitually compare yourself to others and place yourself on the short side of stick, then it's important to explore this way of thinking. There's a lot of *me* in the thought: He has more expertise on this subject than I and therefore, he's better than I; I may just as well resign from this committee—I'm no use. Sound oversimplified? Some of us find ourselves in this pattern often if we're in the game of comparing ourselves with others. What we don't get so easily is that it's really okay to not be good at every thing.

Whether we place ourselves above or below others, we are substituting an idea about who we or others are or should be for the simple truth that as human beings we are good at some things and not so good at other things. We fail and we succeed. We know and we don't know. We accomplish some useful things and we mess up some other things. This is what it means to be human.

THE PRACTICE

Stop. Look. Listen. Notice the ways you measure yourself to others. As with the other precepts, study your actions, words, body, and thoughts. You no doubt will find that there are certain favorites and some that are finely tuned for certain people and situations. When you do this inquiry, it's imperative that you work with the situation at hand. It can be any situation in which you catch yourself falling into measuring. Perhaps you find that you secretly wish others would fail. Maybe you look for a situation or person to blame. Perhaps you find that underlying frustration or anger at things not getting done at work is the fact that you have placed yourself above others by trying to do it all—caring for the kids, working, etc. Sometimes we may even set others up to not do well so that we have to come to the rescue. The thinking that I've got to do it or it won't get done not only can ensure us of our importance, but also ends up taking from others the opportunity to do their best. What's more, this type of action can send a message to others that we don't believe they can do it. This *savior* thinking, however, puts us in a bind because then we have to do whatever it is we have taken on ourselves. If it's something we have time for or like to do, no problem, but if not, then we may feel put upon or angry, and may think, Why me?

Watch how your thoughts create a story about people rather than letting them reveal themselves. At some point you'll be able to catch it every now and again before you begin to do it.

Now experience what it's like to engage without the story. This needn't be just with new people, but can be with your partner, your kids, anyone you've known for a long time.

Try meeting them as if for the first time—as strangers, just as in the last precept. Turn your attention to their physical characteristics. What is the color of their eyes? Look at their faces as if you were seeing them for the first time.

Listen to what they're saying and how they're saying it— the words, the pauses, and the voice intonation. This is not as difficult as it may seem. It's simply a matter of turning your attention toward what is in front of you, not what's in your head. No story, just what is.

As you find your thoughts going off into a story line, return again and again to the person in front of you while staying in touch with the feelings or sensations that may arise.

Deepening the Inquiry

Relax into the Dead Spot

Now you can ask yourself, spiraling deeper in the practice, What is the worst thing that could happen if I wasn't better than . . . ? Relax and settle into the question like an old sweater. This is the place of the dead spot. Don't push or demand and answer, but try to maintain openness so that the answer simply rises forth into your consciousness. Somewhere deep inside ourselves, we know the intention of our actions; we just don't know that we know it. So this type of question is really an invitation for us to listen deeply. It is not a demand, and above all it's not a test. The answer may come immediately, or it may take days, weeks, or months of bringing our attention over and over to what it feels like when that possibility arises.

Listen to and feel your feelings and body sensations. Whatever your experience is, just let it rise naturally, breathing in and out. Let the thoughts about your experience melt into the experiencing itself as you breathe. In this place without comparison, you stand alone and present to the fullness of all that you are.

CONVERSATIONS

Student: I'm still not clear on how measuring ourselves as less than relates to this precept.

Diane: Does anyone want to respond?

Student: When I was working with this particular precept, I made a practice that every time I found myself sitting with a group of people—in the train on my way to work, in the meditation hall, in a meeting at work—I would go around the room, person by person, and observe how I experienced myself in relation to that person. I only spent about thirty seconds on each individual. What I realized after doing this practice for a time was that whether I experienced myself as better than or less than, the comparison always put *me* absolutely at the center, in my own mind, of what everyone else was doing. As long as I was measuring, I was leaving others out.

Another Student: It makes you the yardstick by which everybody else is measured.

Diane: Exactly.

Another Student: The ridiculous thing is that I bet a lot of other people in those situations are doing exactly the same thing.

Diane: And we wonder why we're all so confused.

Another Student: Working with this precept really blew my cover. One of my requirements is that I always need to do the *right* thing. This is how I measure myself in relation to others. *Right,* in my book, means doing and saying *good* things. I found it slippery and subtle because I'm pretty good at speaking and acting in ways that make me look good to others. So it isn't about the overt so much as the covert. After some time, I began to realize that much of my identity is boosted by manipulating the way I speak.

For example, I'm good at letting people hear what they want to hear. So the practice became noticing when I was doing this and inquiring what might be behind some of that requirement. I noticed more and more the need to be validated, the need to be liked, the need to be seen as having no faults, the investment I had in some people being perceived negatively, and so on. I measured myself accordingly. I also started seeing how, without directly saying something negative about someone else, the way I put something could lead the person I was speaking to to draw some negative conclusions about someone else. Of course this made me look better. It's all so subtle; I know I still miss a lot. Plus I find it painful to see because it necessitates being aware that I did some harm, or that I have investment in people seeing that I do good. But I know this is a critical practice for me because this particular way of being is like the air I breathe. It's so subtle and slippery. I sense that this practice is unraveling something at the cellular level.

The Perfection of Being Neither Better nor Worse

"Like the air I breathe . . . subtle and slippery." This student's words describe so well both the intensity and character of our reactionary patterns. We believe them to the marrow of our bones. But we don't have to spend the remainder of our lives living that way. We are perfect as we are even if we don't experience ourselves or others in that way. As the poet Rilke reminds us: "take your practiced powers and stretch them out until they span the chasm between contradictions . . . for the god wants to know himself in you." [2]

And that's what our practice with this precept offers us—the opportunity to truly experience perfection as neither better nor worse, bigger or smaller, than anything else in the universe. And then slowly, over time, inquiring into and slowly deconstructing our patterns of measuring ourselves to others, we can have moments when we truly meet each other on equal ground. But like the Buddha advises, don't believe this because I say it or because you read it in a book. Believe only your own experience. That's why we practice. It takes a lot of courage. It takes a lot of patience. It takes a lot of tenacity to do this kind of work. It isn't something we can learn by listening to a talk and then just believing it.

EIGHT

I Take Up the Way of Cultivating a Clear Mind

Each Moment, life as it is—the only Teacher.
—"Practice Principles" recited at the
Ordinary Mind Zen School

I've heard it said that 90 percent of getting along well in life is in showing up for it. I'd add to that thought—showing up fully *in each moment*. Being present is not just being present in body alone but in body *and* clear mind. This precept, sometimes worded as Not Giving or Taking Drugs, Not Indulging in Intoxicants, or Not Clouding the Truth, encourages us to take an honest look at the ways we don't show up by clouding our experience through the use of intoxicating substances and addictive behaviors. We may acknowledge at some level that all the moments of our lives are teachers, but we don't always want to meet the teacher, so sometimes we seek to control or regulate our experience in a variety of ways. This is a form of escape that not only can lead us into further ignorance, but also can lead us to taking actions out of greed and anger. As another of my students phrases it:

> *Fear holds the cup and I hide in the distortion of its shadow. The cup falls and sunlight blinds with painful brightness. I vow to stand with empty hands, tight chest, trembling, and tears. I vow to stand with eyes open to what is revealed. Who drops the cup?*

If we have any hope of being free from the habitual swings of our reactions, if we have any wish to live more openly and freely, if we seek to, as writer Barbara Kingsolver says, "look life in the eye and love it back,"[1] then we need to take a look at what's clouding our view. This is what any teacher offers us—a clear view of our clouding. But in order to even recognize the teacher, we need to be awake. This is, first of all, what this precept is about—being awake and present for our teachers. It points to the ways in which we play hooky or daydream in the back of the class of everyday teachings that present themselves to us as we go about our ordinary activities of living.

Secondly, it directs us toward cultivating the potential clarity we all possess by shining the beacon on the ways we pollute that clarity by the use of substances and other behaviors. One way to think of the mind's innate clarity is by comparing it to rich, unworked soil—full of possibilities and nutrients, teeming with millions of insects, microorganisms, bacteria, and enzymes standing ready in full potential to interact and bring forth whatever seeds are planted there. Much like a gardener carefully cares for the soil by not adding pollutants and toxic substances so that its full potential can nurture and grow the seeds planted, we can cultivate a mind that is rich, open, and ready to cultivate the seeds planted by life's events—our teachers. This precept is not about changing our mind, but rather it's about inquiring into the ways we get lost in obscuring or clouding it. It's about making use of the clarity that is already ours for the taking—the clarity that allows us to cultivate whatever seeds life brings our way.

Originally, this precept focused on the use of alcohol, but later it was expanded to include the use of other substances like marijuana, tranquilizers, hallucinogens, and so forth. Today, we can think of more subtle ways we turn from being present by using and abusing not only mind-altering drugs, but also caffeine, cigarettes, food, and ac-tivities like exercise, TV watching, internet surfing, work, sensory highs, or anything that can turn us from the immediate experience of our minds and bodies. So in exploring this precept, we focus not so much on what particular drugs or activities are *acceptable* to use, but rather what our intention is and how we can use any substance or engage in any activity that drives us further into our habitual ways of meeting the events and circumstances of every day life. My point is that alcohol, drugs, TV, whatever, are not escapes in and of themselves. What makes them escapes is how we use them.

In some traditions, students take this precept as a vow of abstinence. And although in our working with it, we may purposely abstain from certain substances or activities at some point in the inquiry, we do not take the strictly prohibitive view of this precept: Don't drink anything; don't take any drugs. It need not be mentioned that drugs used for medical or psychological conditions may alter the mind, but may be the best course of action for certain conditions, if used wisely and with diligent awareness. Our approach to this precept is not to determine how or to what extent a substance or an activity may cloud or alter our experience, but rather to point to how we may use and abuse them by obscuring the wisdom and intelligence present in life as it is in any event, any moment, and in any place. A cool beer on a hot day is refreshing if we don't have an alcoholic addiction and if we are not using it for any other reason that to be refreshed. Settling down to a good movie on TV can be very relaxing if we aren't, for example, trying to avoid the bills on our desk or our disappointment over losing a job promotion. Ice cream is a tasty treat when we're not eating a quart of it in an effort to sweeten the pain of a breakup with our partner. This precept is about looking at the ways we use whatever substance to alter or escape our experience, in some of the ways I've listed, and many more.

THE PRACTICE

We begin our work by inquiring into the ways in which we may try to control or regulate our thoughts, feelings, and body experiences by tuning out, tuning up, and turning on. I have found the range of experiences of people working with this precept is very wide. Some people never drink or use drugs at all so are convinced at the beginning that they could probably just skip over this one. Others have a history of substance abuse and are scared to death of it. Some have found by first exploring this precept a bit that they are dealing with a much deeper physical addiction than they had realized, and the Enter Here sign above the door directs their way into treatment and recovery. Others come to it after years of recovery and want to explore the deeper patterns of their addictive behavior.

A good way to begin exploring this precept is to pick one substance or activity that you regularly engage in with some attachment (in other words, you'd have some reaction if you couldn't do it), and begin observing yourself internally while using or engaging in that activity.

Deepening the Inquiry

How Many Ways Can One Drink a Glass of Wine?

One person I know is a wine connoisseur. In fact, he hesitated to begin precept work for quite a long time because he thought he would have to give up his hobby of wine collecting (including daydreaming in meditation by mentally rearranging his wine cellar). To begin his practice, he decided to take at least five minutes to sit in silence, observing his mind and body state—agitated, calm, tense, relaxed—before he poured a glass of wine. Five minutes may not seem very long, but when you're keeping yourself from engaging in a habitual form of avoidance, it can seem like an eternity. What he came up with at the end of two weeks was that he could drink a glass of wine in many different ways, depending on what was going on in his thinking as he reached for the glass. Sometimes, he was fully present as he smelled the fullness of the aroma and tasted the layers of flavor passing across his tongue. He said that in those times, he had no thought of taking the next sip or how full his glass was or how much was left in the bottle. His mind and body were pretty level before he began. Other times he had the opposite experience. He experienced tenseness and agitation and could hardly wait to gulp down the first glass.

This insight may seem fairly obvious to the reader, and if my student had talked about it in advance, he probably would have come up with the same insight. But intellectual insights are not what this exercise is about. It's about being awake and present to the full range of the experience as you are engaged in the activity.

Engage the Observer

Try it yourself with your own substance or activity, whatever it may be. Remember the idea here isn't necessarily abstinence. It's exploration. Be open to whatever you experience. Allow it. Say hello. Watch it. Observe it. Get to know it intimately. What does your body really feel like when it has a craving? Feel the physical drive behind switching the channels or surfing the net. Notice what you're thinking or avoiding thinking about. Get to know your escape.

After you've practiced this way for a while and have a sense of what it feels like before, during, and after you have engaged in your preferred method of clouding, you can begin to inquire a little deeper by experimenting with extending your awareness. This is an extension of the practice of sitting for five minutes before engaging in the activity. Now sit for at least five minutes afterward, no matter what your state. This is a lot easier said than done, but it is possible. Another person working with this precept managed to sit for a few minutes even when he came home late one night after partying and was quite drunk. All he remembered the next day was trying to not fall over. But he learned something—even if just how to sit in a meditation position while drunk. It's not so simple, and takes every ounce of awareness you can muster up! Whether it's food, alcohol, exercise, or whatever route of exit you take, you can find your way back by turning toward your body awareness. What is the sensation as you pause five minutes before opening the refrigerator door? What are the thoughts and feelings after you shut it? What about when you place the used dishes in the sink after you've finished eating or drinking?

Another person I know, a recovering heroin addict, was faced with the necessity of taking painkillers after a painful surgery. Fearful of introducing drugs into his system again, he fretted for months over what to do and even postponed a much-needed surgery. He knew he was headed for treacherous waters and even though the lighthouse beacon was clear and precise, he had no choice but to stay on course even though he wanted to avoid it at all costs. He explored many modes of pain reduction, but finally acknowledged that he would need barbiturates. So his practice with this precept was to take the drugs and stay in close contact as much as possible to what was happening as he experienced the drug take effect. Sometimes this is all we can do. We do not always have the control we think we have. And this is where we can find our teacher.

After the surgery was completed and as he observed himself over the next few weeks as he monitored his pain and decided on the appropriate dosage of medication, he found that he needed to muster up every ounce of observation he could. Then he began to uncover a very deeply held requirement—he needed to be in control. He realized that under his addiction from the beginning—first with marijuana, then with alcohol, and later cocaine and heroin—he was not simply trying to alter his experience, thus avoiding the fear and anger that were cultivated early in his life; by altering his experience, he believed he was controlling what he felt helpless to face. Even after years of counseling and recovery work, this teacher wasn't finished with him. He now had to face the fact that he was not and could not always be in control. In Alcoholics Anonymous twelve-step language, he was back to step one: Admitting I am powerless. He asked himself then, Who is this "I" that is powerless?

Wonderful question! And he had found yet his next teacher.

Ever Changing, Ever Clouding

What becomes clear after we've observed ourselves in action around this precept is that the crystal clarity of the mind inevitably gets clouded over. This is quite natural. It's the human condition. We may be able to cease the clouding caused by imbibing certain substances and engaging in certain activities, but the clouding of mind is inevitable as we go about our lives as thinking, physical beings. This is what people who rarely imbibe mind-altering substances or engage in other activities that cloud the perceptions learn from this precept. We need to think in order get from one side of a room to another to answer the doorbell, or to turn the pages of this book. As one Zen master reminds us, the pure, immaculate mind of Just This moment is clouded in the nanosecond of every thought. So in a certain sense, we become intoxicated every time we have a thought. Being that we need to think as functioning human beings, we are therefore always intoxicated. When we consume substances or engage in activities to alter our experience, we just become more "drunk"!

As well, our brains are drug factories producing thousands of substances that course through our bodies, regulating our moods and behaviors. Melatonin produced in a daily rhythm induces sleep. Adrenaline is produced in response to danger, which causes blood to be diverted to muscles in preparation for action, and an extreme level of alertness. Even drugs that we consume voluntarily often have their effect by virtue of their similarity to neurotransmitters, the natural chemical messengers that travel back and forth between neurons in your brain, carrying messages between the brain and the rest of the body. Endorphins are typically released in high dosages when we're in some kind of pain and are well known as "runner's high." Seratonin release is associated with mood and is now used for the treatment of depression. These substances occur naturally but can also be manipulated by drugs, exercise, food, and, indeed, many activities we engage in.

So what are we to do? As my friend who found he must take barbiturates for his surgery learned, the purpose of this precept, as with all the precepts, is to cultivate the clarity that keeps us alert and present so that we more quickly catch our swings on the habitual patterns of our reactions. The value of working with this precept is not to try to clear the clouds away forever, but to come to understand that neither the clouds alone nor the clear blue sky alone is the fullness of life. They arise and fall away as part of being human. Our intention is to know them as best we can and to not be attached to one or the other. Through our practice we can have opening experiences, when all thinking and the dream of self falls away completely, but the phone will ring, the kids will need to be picked up at school, bills need to be paid, more dirty dishes appear in the sink, and we'll have our reactions to them—the clouds will reappear. The real question is: Do we catch them before we swing into action?

CONVERSATIONS

Student: It strikes me how much we're steeped in a culture that constantly sends out messages that some mind or body experiences are okay while others are not. For example, it's okay to be on the go and active with unlimited energy, but not okay to get tired. I'm thinking about simple things like energy bars or energy drinks that we consume throughout the day to keep on going. It's like the message is peak experience is the best experience, that there's something wrong if we want to slow down because we're tired. I sometimes wonder how all of this is tied into the larger value system of our culture of more is better.

Diane: It's no surprise that what we put into our mouths reflects what's in our heads. Maybe it is a reflection of our society. It's interesting to think about this, but we need to look to our own intention. The real practice comes in how we handle body or mind states we're not satisfied with— that don't meet the requirements we have come to rely on in order to avoid more core beliefs about who we think we are. If I have a deadline to meet, and I'm clean out of energy, I'll no doubt reach for a piece of chocolate or a cup of coffee. Remember, it's not the substance; it's our intention in using it and the harm and suffering it causes when we use it to cloud our ability to take clear, intelligent action.

Student: As I work with this precept I realize that I have expectations that I *should* experience certain feelings around certain situations. For example, I *should* feel happy when I get home from work at night and see my partner and kids. When I don't, I often reach for a beer or glass of wine so that I can relax and loosen up in order to enjoy them more. I know my intention is to relax, but would that be such a bad thing to do if it allows me to be there and enjoy my family more? Would you call this an addiction?

Diane: But are you really there? Would there be another way to be there and honor the tenseness, rather than ignoring it? This is what your practice can offer you. There are a lot of ways to talk about addiction. There is a physical addiction at a cellular level, in which the organism comes to crave certain substances. This is the level of addiction of the drug addict or alcoholic. Then there's a more general way of talking about addiction, much like what you might be describing here. I think of addiction in this way as a requirement that causes us to act in body, speech, and mind in a certain way in order to alter our experience. What is your requirement here?

Student: That I always be relaxed and enjoy coming home and being with my family.

Diane: And is that true? Are you always relaxed when you come home and do you always enjoy being with your family when you come home?

Student: No.

Diane: Where is it written that you must always be relaxed and enjoy your family? This question is your point of entry. You've observed yourself in action, now you circle into the next spiral. Grab this question with your life—before you reach for the bottle of beer. You'll learn something. I don't know what that will be. This is your discovery. Own it. Your addiction is your requirement—not the beer or wine.

Requirements viewed as addictions reveal how we narrow our awareness and form a rigidity of mind, thus cutting off our awareness of the natural flow of life. When we insist that our experience of any event must be a certain way, this is a form of addiction. When we are afraid to let go of the habitual bars of reaction to rest in the moment open and available to whatever comes up, this is addiction, and it closes us off from the juice of life.

Student: So what would the nonaddictive state be?

Diane: The moments when we realize that we do not have to fulfill the requirements we insist on hanging onto. The addictive state *requires* life/me/others be a certain way. The nonaddictive state is free, open, wide, *receiving* life/me/others as they are. It is the place of the open heart.

Student: And does it include our resistance to all of the above?

Diane: Yes! Indeed!

Student: This precept often includes not giving drugs to others. Can you talk more about this?

Diane: We can talk about a wide range of participation in others clouding their awareness. But equally important is how we help others cultivate a clear mind. The most obvious ways in which we contribute to others clouding their awareness is manufacturing, growing, and/or distributing substances with the intention of simply giving them to whoever wants it. This, of course, doesn't include actions like growing marijuana or other drugs for medical use only. I realize as a society, we're all over the map on this issue, but what's important, again, is what our intention is and how much are we willing to look our responsibility in the eye. Does the grower know in whose hands—a grown adult, or a confused adolescent—the drugs he sells to the buyer will land? The web of interconnection is not so clearly defined. It would be difficult to separate ourselves completely from the ways we contribute to others' misuse of anything. In the same way, should we place fault on the liquor companies, or the neighbor who works in the local liquor store to support her family, because some people use liquor as a way to avoid life as it is? Of course not, but it does remind us of the inevitable complicity we play in each other's lives. For example, sometimes I think about the children in classrooms I've visited as a learning therapist whose behavior was modified by the use of drugs to calm them down and help them concentrate. Of course the teachers', parents', and doctors' intentions were well meant, but I wonder how many times these children were being treated in order to mold their individual energies and spontaneity to the needs of their parents' busy schedule or teachers' overloaded classroom.

But equally important here is how we engage in actions that can help others to cultivate a clear mind. The best way to do this, as always, is to set an example. Coming home tense and tired after a day's work, instead of reaching for the beer in the refrigerator, would it be possible to take a few minutes to sit quietly alone by yourself with the full experience of your thoughts and bodily sensations? Think about what that would teach your kids. And if you don't have kids or if you live alone, it still has enormous effect in the *family of things*.

Sometimes helping others is not as easy as changing your own behavior. Sometimes it takes every bit of courage and strength we can muster because it brings us face to face with our deepest fears.

Some years ago I realized that someone very dear to me had a severe drinking addiction. After having experienced this with my first husband, it took me some time to acknowledge that this was happening again and to acknowledge that I was not in control. Sending this person money for rent, trying to do all the things I could in an effort to avoid facing the reality of the situation, was not working. My loved one was steadily going downhill—dangerously so. I had attended Alanon meetings where I learned about the courage and strength of the human spirit as I listened to friends, mothers, fathers, sons, and daughters speak of how they confronted the truth of their loved ones' addictions. They spoke of seeing them in jail, finding them sleeping in garbage containers, all the worst scenarios one could think of. But I had not yet met my own teacher. That came one cold February day when I received a desperate telephone call from New England where the temperature was reaching below freezing. I was once again being asked for money, this time to pay rent to avoid eviction and be left in the freezing temperatures with no place to go. As I listened to the words coming through the telephone receiver, something happened to me. I remembered, as a distant echo, something I'd read years ago, something about "for a human being . . . there is no other way of life than this way of life." The seed had sprouted. Suzuki Roshi's words, which I had read several years earlier as I happened on his book on my coffee table, struck clear to my consciousness. *This life* is my life. *This life* is the life of my dear one. And so I had to release him to his own life. And, perhaps, even death. I could not save him nor could I reach his bottom for him. So I responded, "I cannot send you money this time. Deep down, I think you know why. If your landlady evicts you and you are in the street, then you might try going to an AA meeting or to another type of shelter." Was it easy? Of course not, even with Suzuki Roshi's wise words. My voice trembled and I was near panic. Without a word, he hung up and I was not to hear again from him for nearly a year. Today this person has been clean and sober for nearly fifteen years, but both he and I remember the wise advice: take each day, each moment at a time. This is your life. It's all you've got. So live yours to the fullest by looking it in the eye, and do what you can to help others do the same, and so the chain continues. There are no guarantees that things will work out without pain. Another person in another time and place may respond very differently. I am not suggesting that my action is always the only appropriate action. Perhaps the action that best serves life in another situation would be to send the money. What I am saying, however, is that this precept directs us toward cultivating clarity of intent—being crystal clear about what is behind our actions, even actions to help others toward clarity.

MORE CONVERSATIONS

Student: I know you've been waiting for this question: Through the history of humankind, people have used drugs to open the door to spiritual experiences. Would that be considered using substances to cloud awareness?

Diane: You're right, I was wondering when this one would come along! Yes, there is no doubt that there's evidence that altered mind states and opening of perception can be experienced with substances. Recently, I read in a scientific journal about a study of gasses that scientists found evidence of in the rocks at the site of the Delphic oracle in Greece. The gas, ethylene, at low concentrations can induce a trance state. People using LSD and other drugs of this century report similar mind-expanding experiences. More recently, drugs like Ecstasy have been used to relieve inhibitions, enabling the user to feel more open and connected to others. Let's not forget, though, that with any of these and other drugs, many people, and not just the users, have been hurt. Even at Delphi, the danger of death by going into the cave of gases was well known. How many people today have permanent brain and body damage because they were seeking alternate mind states? As I mentioned earlier, my purpose of discussion here is not to argue the merits or demerits of any substance, be it marijuana, Ecstasy, or caffeine. What I do want to emphasize is that what it comes down to is, are we looking for a short-lived experience or are we looking for transformation? Many substances can open the door, but as soon as the high is over, the door slams shut, and you're just you again. Cultivating a clear mind doesn't mean we get rid of anything or try to transcend anything. It just means we *look life in the eye*. And in that direct meeting, we come to experience a clarity and wonder that is ours for the taking. We do not need outside substances. Be assured. Your life will go on. The question is, will you show up?

NINE

I Take Up the Way of Taking Only What Is Freely Given and Giving Freely of All That I Can

> Giving and receiving are at bottom one thing,
> dependent upon whether one lives open or closed.
> Living openly one becomes a medium, a transmit-
> ter; living thus, as a river, one experiences life to
> the full, flows along with the current of life, and
> dies in order to live again as an ocean.
> —Henry Miller, *The Colossus of Maroussi*[1]

We live in a complicated world of give and take. It doesn't take much effort working with this precept to realize that taking what isn't ours to take includes far more than stealing another person's wallet or embezzling money from the company we work for. It includes more subtle forms of taking what is not ours to take, like cheating on our taxes or in taking exams; making illegal copies of music, video, and audiotapes; padding the bills for service. It includes raping the environment of natural resources because we think we *own* the oil, timber, and minerals of the earth. The list grows quite long when we consider that stealing, to a larger extent than what any of us might want to acknowledge, drives the intricacies of our social and economical system—and what we believe, beyond our basic needs, is *enough*. Someone asked a CEO of a very successful investment company, "How much do you make?" The CEO answered with a knowing smile, "I make the same as everyone else—not enough!" As I mentioned previously, one of my students expresses this precept this way:

> *At times when I feel I am entitled to what others*
> *want, need, or own, I resolve to hold this hard ball*
> *of entitlement, of separation, to feel its texture, and*
> *to wait until its nature is clear.*

The second part of this precept, *giving freely of all that I can,* also includes far more than we may think. It includes more than how much money we give each year in charity; it reaches much further into how open we are with the *spirit* of giving our time, energy, talents, and commitment. It reflects how much time we take to stop and talk to a person who looks like he can use a friendly word; how much time we're willing to help out in ways that don't directly affect us. As the words of Henry Miller point out, giving and taking are not unrelated. In fact, the universe is engaged in a reciprocal dance of give and take. We cannot have one without the other.

Let us begin by taking a look at the many different ways we take what is not freely given and exploring our beliefs about what we think we don't have, what we think we should have, and what we have. Sometimes the first half of this precept is worded as a prohibition against stealing, but the core of this precept goes deeper than just taking what is not ours to take. It invites us to consider deeply what and how we ask or don't ask for whatever it is we want or need. It invites us to consider how we give or don't offer what we are capable of giving. It then leads us into a deeper inquiry into notions of lacking and deserving—beliefs that we require and deserve to have more than what we do have.

At the most basic level, we can think about taking what is not freely given as taking anything that is not ours to take—taking another's property without permission—material goods, money, ideas, works of arts. This type of taking ranges from armed robbery to letting slide a cashier's mistake at the checkout counter in your favor by not saying, "Excuse me, I think there is an error in the calculation. I need to pay more." Cheating and larceny are other forms of stealing, and share borders with lying. People cheat on their taxes, on exams, on their partners. All can be explored as a form of theft.

Then there's the common stealing that goes along with the idea that if it's there for the taking, then take it. How many napkins do you grab with that take-out coffee? Or what about pocketing those extra sugar or marmalade packets in the restaurant? What about using the office phone for making personal charge calls or taking an hour of company time to do some personal business?

By extension, we can also explore ways we extend this kind of thinking into the environment, assuming that because it's there, it's ours for the taking. Do we really need a sign on the steering wheel of our car that reads "Can I walk to where I'm going?" to remind us to use less oil? The same holds true for leaving the lights on in a room after we've left it or throwing paper in the trash instead of recycling. It takes presence of mind to even notice the light is on as we leave a room. This is difficult to do if our thoughts have raced six steps outside the door before our hand reaches the doorknob.

Once we begin to wake up a bit to what we're taking simply because it's available, it becomes clear that taking only what is freely given is freedom to take what is needed, not license to take all that we can. We take all sorts of things from others—time, attention, and even life's lessons. How might we intervene when life offers a valuable lesson to our children? And behind it all, of course, is what do we get out of it?

At a more subtle level, this precept directs us to the door marked "Getting Something." It encourages us to meet the beliefs, assumptions, and habitual thought patterns behind that door that fuel our insistence on getting what we want. It leads us to uncovering the mind of *attainment*. And quite often, what fuels this need for attainment is the belief of *not-enough-ness, insufficiency, lack*. The form this belief takes is different for all of us. It may be fueled by a belief of entitlement—being owed more than what you're receiving. It may be fueled by the belief that life will not support you, is not enough—that you are incomplete, vulnerable, small, and powerless. This precept offers us the opportunity to meet the world, our partners, our neighbors and friends, our children, and ourselves beyond these patterns of thinking, recognizing the generosity, gratitude, fullness, and abundance of life in the most ordinary gestures of going about our daily activities.

Crying Over Spilled Milk

Once there was a struggling single mother who sent one of her three daughters to the corner store to get some milk. On the way home, the girl's shoe caught in a crack in the pavement and as she stumbled, she dropped the carton of milk, spilling half of it onto the ground. She returned home crying, feeling clumsy, inadequate, and guilty, reporting to her mother that there was now only half a carton of milk.

The next day, the mother sent another one of her other daughters on the same errand. And once again, the child tripped on the cracked pavement, spilling half the milk onto the ground. But this child had a different take on the spill. She peeked inside the carton and saw that it was still half full. She returned happy, proud that she was able to save as much as she did and sure that the loss of the milk would not make a difference at home. She told her mother that she tripped but was able to save half the milk.

On the final day, the mother sent her last daughter to buy the milk for the day. The city still hadn't fixed the crack in the pavement and the girl tripped, spilling half of the milk on the ground. Like her sisters, the girl picked up the carton with the remainder of the milk in it and continued on. But this daughter had a different view of what was left in the carton. First, she muttered a little "darn it!" as she observed a wave of anger pass quickly through her awareness. Then she looked inside the carton and thought, "Hmmm. There's about half gone and there's about half still there." On her way home she thought about the implications of the situation and the best way to deal with it. When she arrived home, she said to her mother, "I am sorry, but like my sisters, I tripped over the crack in the pavement and lost half the milk. If we're very careful how we use it, each of us taking a little less, then we might have enough to get us through the day. But right now, I must go call the city streets department and report the dangerous crack in the pavement so that others don't fall and hurt themselves. "

This is the old half empty, half full idea, often used as a description of optimistic and pessimistic views of life. The half full view is usually considered the best view, but as the above rendition suggests, what's best is not simply a measurement of how full or how empty. It is really both. There is not only scarcity, as the first daughter perceived, nor is there only abundance, as the second daughter suggests. The third view includes a wider view of the situation, including not only what is the best course of action to take given the situation, but also the notion that someone else could be hurt and the authorities need to be alerted to the hole in the sidewalk. The first two daughters react to the event of the spilled milk from their habitual patterns of thinking, while the third meets the situation in the dead spot— between swings of the bar—and takes the action that best serves life. We lose and we gain. We take and we give.

Whose Blossom?

As I was writing this book, I sometimes struggled with finding my words. Echoes of voices I've read and those of my teachers and students found their way into my thoughts and sentences. At first, I became concerned, questioning ownership—which words were theirs, which were mine? But then I realized that even their words could not have sprung up on their own. The seeds in our vegetable garden do not blossom by themselves. Those little green shoots poking their way through the dark earth are the result of their unique potential but also of the sun, the rain, the microbes and enzymes, and our efforts in cultivating and maintaining the soil. Where is the ownership of the blossom? So too, what words find their way into this book are mine but not mine. When it is clear that I am borrowing from another, I give credit by acknowledging the source. But when it is unclear where to draw the line, I receive the words and I give them back freely.

Sometimes when people work with this precept, they find that it leads them to the revelation that not taking what is not freely given relates to their unwillingness to receive what may be offered freely. How many of us shy away from accepting thanks, love, intimacy, help from someone who truly offers it? What automatic refusals arise in the face of an extended hand? And what happens when we don't allow ourselves to receive? What happens to our ability to say "I would like" or "I would not like" if we do not allow the option of receiving?

THE PRACTICE

Begin to notice the obvious and subtle ways in which you take what is not yours to take or ways in which you hold back from giving freely all that you can. Include not just material items, but also time, attention, and so forth. You may notice only obvious things in the beginning—it can take a while to catch some of the subtleties.

One of the difficulties in this first part of the exploration is that what is freely being offered to you or by you is not always so clear. It's pretty clear in the case of the cashier who makes a mistake in your favor and you don't tell her, or when you take company time to do personal business. It's also clear when you ignore a person on the street in obvious need of your help, or when you don't meet your financial responsibilities when you have the resources to do so. But as we go about our lives, it takes a little more intention to stop, look, and listen.

At work, notice how long you take for lunch, coffee, or bathroom breaks, if you take a few supplies for home use, if you take a friend to lunch and put it on your expense account. At home, notice what you might indirectly take from your roommate, partner, or kids, such as time or attention. In the last precept, I mentioned that sometimes we indirectly aid others in clouding awareness. Similarly, we also can steal life's teachers from our children or loved ones under the guise of trying to protect them. This was what I realized when I made the difficult decision to tell my friend that I could not send him the money for his rent. I knew his only chance was for me to get out of the way of the lessons only he could learn. The way to give was to not give.

Deepening the Inquiry

Under the Microscope

In order to begin the process of observing your actions at a closer magnification, choose one or two specific actions and get to know them better, put them under your careful observation. One person I know decided to use her time in the car as she drove back and forth from work as a point of entry into this precept. When in traffic or approaching a tollbooth, she began to notice ways in which she accelerated her speed in order to grab a space in front of her so that another car trying to enter her lane couldn't get in. She watched the way she pressed her foot on the accelerator or manipulated her driving to grab a parking space from another driver. She didn't bring her attention to her driving in order to change it, but rather to try to watch it as an observer—you might say, as a back seat driver, but one who doesn't make comments. Not long into this practice, she found that the awareness stayed with her as she went into the office and interacted with her coworkers. She says:

> After I had been observing my trip to work each day for a while, I realized that a sense of urgency continued as I competed for a parking spot, wormed my way into first place on the elevator, tried to beat others to the coffee machine. I began to understand that that the urgency I experienced as a tingling rush in my chest accompanied by short, quick breathing, had something to do with thoughts such as, if I don't get it, then. . . . Then what? That question began to take hold. What did I think would be the worst thing that could happen if I didn't get that space in front of the car next to me? What is the worst thing that could happen if I wasn't first on the elevator? Of course I could answer these questions logically and would see that nothing very dreadful would happen, but nevertheless, the concern was compelling me into a sense of urgency that propelled me into a sort of tunnel vision in which all I was aware of was what I thought I needed. What's more, the longer I stayed with the experience, feeling this need to take, the less I could find something I really needed to be urgent about.

This is an important point—the difference between *wanting* and *needing*. Sometimes these words are used carelessly. We might say, "I *need* you to give me a space in line," when what we really mean is "I *want* you to give me a space in line." Sometimes we need; sometimes we just want or would like. Let's not confuse the two. Each has its place under specific conditions. When we know the difference, then we are free to take and free to give. But when not used in ways that fit the situation, can my unnecessary need actually limit another's legitimate need, limiting her option to say *no* or *yes* or *maybe?*

We should not speak glibly about need versus want here. This is an important point and one that we should all consider as we face the rising numbers of homeless families both in the United States and around the world. Swollen bellies and wounds of exposure scream out loud and clear— *lack and need.* I'd steal a loaf of bread in a wink if I had no money and I knew it would ward off starvation for myself or my children. But what we're talking about here is a different hunger. It is not a need arising out of basic survival. Rather, we're talking about a hunger that grows out of a misunderstanding that the self is separate and lacking in some basic way. It is a poverty of mind that grows out of perceiving one's self as lacking. It's a poverty in which we convince ourselves that life leaves us out because others have more than we do and we feel compelled to get our share. It is the mind of lacking that gives rise to envy, desire, greed, and a closed heart.

What Is Missing?

For another person practicing with this precept, the precept evolved into the question: What is missing? He came to the following realization:

> It's a lot easier to see what I think is missing than to see what's right in front of me. It's like I'm addicted

to seeing myself as a work in progress, whereby I need to be more successful, more this, or less that. When I've explored being present in this experience of lack, it turns to fear. I sense the fear that if I don't desire and hold onto lack, then I'm lost. It's like a need to hold onto the notion of lacking so that I'll keep on trying to make up for it. That's my requirement. Without it, I have nothing but the core deception that I'm nothing. And that's really scary. But after practicing with this for some time, slowly I've come to feel a little more at ease in this fear. Some days it's easier than others, but strangely enough, it's becoming more okay. It's not so much that the fear is dissipating, but I seem to believe it less.

This belief that we are lacking something, if we believe it so thoroughly, must arise out of the assumption that there is something to attain. This assumption is really the core of this precept. When we are fully awake and present to Just This, then our minds are full, and there can be no thoughts of lacking because there can be nothing that we need to attain. The carton is completely half filled with milk and completely half unfilled with milk—just as it is.

Attainment plays a pervasive and sometimes destructive role in our lives. We live in a world that judges us by what we have attained and we are often impressed by people's positions and acquisitions. This is not limited to the material world but also to the spiritual world. Many people want to attain enlightenment, understanding, to get something out of their spiritual practice that is believed to be lacking. The mind that insists on seeing the cup half empty is the mind that will habitually see most things as empty. There will never be enough.

We also live in a world where many believe it is acceptable to take at will natural resources to satisfy an insatiable appetite that rises with the mind of lack and need. I ask again: want, or need? The earth gives its resources freely, and we often take them without much wisdom. My need to have my living room always heated to seventy degrees quickly becomes a need for the power company serving me to burn more energy for heat, which in turn requires my government to provide more oil, which in turn ties into multibillion-dollar profits in the hands of a few, which in turn, in turn, in turn. . . . We are even willing to topple governments and go to war to satisfy these needs. This is why it is important for us to look deeply into what motivates our actions when we take what is not freely given.

The mind of lacking also extends to our feelings about ourselves. Another of my students found an interesting twist as she explored her need for others to affirm her worthiness:

> Instead of being responsible for my own behavior, I've found that I sometimes use other people's opinions to define myself. I steal and demand other people's judgments of my behavior by demanding from them what I can only realize for myself. I seek out their approval and their disapproval as a way of determining who I am. By seeking what is not freely given I can take the easy out. I'm off the hook. I can avoid feeling what I'm really feeling by paying attention to them and their opinions rather than observing my own actions and emotions. Instead of getting mad over not being able to get something right I can get upset over their perceived judgment of me "doing something wrong." This became apparent to me during my last aikido class when I noticed that when I don't understand a new

move and can't do it, I make comments about "What a klutz I am," "How can you stand working with me," in hopes that my sparring partner will tell me that I'm working hard and that I'm okay. I want him to redeem me by forgiving me for not getting it right. What I realize is that I'm wanting from him what I can only give to myself, and I'm willing to manipulate ways to take what I think I must have.

Three-Letter-Word Practice: But *or* And

Another useful practice to help us turn toward recognizing abundance is simply substituting the word *and* for the word *but*. People often say things to me like, "I try to listen more openly to my kids *but* I get so angry with them," or "I want to do this or be that way, *but* . . ." The word *but* expresses the mind of exclusion. It separates, leaves out, censors what is. The word *and* includes. Whatever our experience—"I try to listen more openly to my kids *and* I get so angry with them," or "I want to do this or be that way, *and* . . . "—these two, small, three-letter words can be the difference between having an open or a closed heart.

Practice listening to yourself when you speak. Notice when and under what conditions you use the words *but* or *and*. You may find this a little difficult to catch at first, *and* if you are persistent you will find that you'll catch yourself more easily. When you find that you are using *but* as a way to censor or exclude a thought, immediately rephrase that thought substituting the word *and* for *but*.

The closed heart rises out of the belief that whatever uncomfortable condition arises in our lives, it doesn't belong. The closed heart picks and chooses what it will let in and out. If something poses no threat to the self-centered dream, then it's let in. But if it does pose a threat, it's closed out. A truly open heart, however, has no hinges to open and close because the truly open heart knows no door.

Another way to think of this practice is to imagine a large circle. The circle is life itself. It includes enough and not enough, giving and taking, living and dying, war and peace, joy and heartache, what is and what isn't, form and emptiness—the full spectrum of all conditions. *But* places the condition presenting itself out side the circle. *And* welcomes it in. One closes; the other opens.

What's Your Price Tag?

True giving has no attachments. It flows along with the current of life. But giving can be confusing and manipulative if we give with a price tag attached. There is no freedom in this type of giving. The heart is not open, but closing in on what it can get in return. Price tags have different costs—to be appreciated, to be seen as generous and caring, to stash aside favors owed us. The price tag says, "I give, but you pay back. Now you owe me." Anytime we find ourselves having some type of reaction after we've given money, items, time, attention, even our love, and not received something in return, then we know we have attached a price tag. Bringing awareness to this pattern of giving can shine the beacon on how we define ourselves and others.

Last week while in line at the grocery store, I let a young man go ahead of me since he had just one item and I had a cartful of items. The initial gesture on my part seemed simply practical, but when he failed to say "thank you," I found myself making judgments about not only him, but many young people and parents who don't teach their children how to say thank you and so on. . . . . I realized that there was just a whisper of a thought before I gave him the place ahead of me in line that went something like, Look at me, aren't I a good person to be doing this?

This precept reminds us that nothing is lacking in any of our experiences. When we begin to see our habitual ways of taking, not taking, holding, giving, not giving, we can be open, even if only very briefly, to all there is. I am not talking about a naïve "the cup is always half full" view, but a realization that goes far beyond a philosophical perspective. When we first recognize our habitual trapeze swings, we also see how limited our view is in terms of what's available to us. The woman who was observing her driving noticed after just a few round-trips from her home to work not only how often she cut people off, but also how often people tried to speed up so as to not let her in, and how often people slowed down to make space for her.

Acts of Kindness

Within the Buddhist tradition, generosity of giving, *dana*, is an important practice. But *dana* is not practiced simply as giving to others just to be of help. Giving openly can also have a profound effect on the many ways we can open a heart that has been closed because of anger, jealousy, fear, or rejection. It can stop the reactionary pattern of taking in its tracks and turn taking into giving. One student expresses it this way:

> If I were to give without expectation; if I were to accept without judgment; if I were to experience just this moment without rushing impatiently to the next; then . . . ?

Several years ago a popular bumper sticker appeared on people's cars. It read: "Practice Random Acts of Kindness." What the message was suggesting was to do something generous without calculation or expected payback. For example, you could leave a note of appreciation and thanks to the mailperson or the garbage collector. Imagine what impact that could have on our world—a world of people saying "thank you!" Or you could visit an elderly neighbor for a few minutes. There are numerous acts of random kindness that one could think up. Try doing something every day for your housemate or a friend or a neighbor. It can be as simple as picking up your roommate's clothes off the floor and hanging them in the closet. It could be taking in your neighbor's trash cans or sweeping the front of her house. Standing in line at the grocery store, stand back as you and another person are about to enter the checkout line and let him go first. And what do you discover when you give and no one knows but yourself? Notice how you feel when you engage in giving openly. How do you feel when you say thank you or someone else gives thanks to you?

One person I know was having conflicts with someone at work. He said all he could think of when he saw her was all the ways she's make his life at work miserable. He practiced hard, experiencing the anger, feeling the heat in his chest, labeling the thoughts, and opening to the deeper fears her actions were generating in him, and then he decided to go one step more. He decided to make a simple gesture of giving each day as a way to counter the pattern of his thinking. Each day he would do one thing for her— ask her if she wanted a cup of coffee on his way to the coffee machine. Bend over and pick up something she dropped, and so forth. These actions may seem minor, but these simple acts of giving are powerful.

To practice *giving freely of all that you can* does not mean to empty your house of all its belongings. It doesn't even mean that you have to swing open your heart, letting go of all your defenses at once. It means to first come to know your resistance to giving and then to give what you can within that moment. Then every day, just do one thing that goes against that pattern of holding back and see what your experience is when you open in that way.

What's Wrong with Your Bike?

Not long ago I read a true story in *The International Herald Tribune* newspaper about a young woman who was a Peace Corps volunteer in Burkina Faso, a small country in western Africa. Riding her bicycle over an eighteen-kilometer country road, she hit a bump and fell to the ground, damaging her bike so that she could not pedal. With seven more kilometers to the nearest town, she sat in disbelief on the ground, sun blazing, 115-degree heat, and only half a liter of water left in her canteen. "Great," she muttered as she began pushing her bike down the path.

Minutes later she spotted an older man coming on his bike from the opposite direction. *"Yaa boe tara fo weefo?"* he asked her in Moore, the language of the Mossi people, "What's wrong with your bike?" After she explained to him what had happened, he took a look at probably the first twenty-one-speed bike he had ever seen and, flashing a smile, said he couldn't fix it but "we'll find some other way." He proceeded to hook up a rubber strap to her handlebars and connected it to his old bike. Dumbfounded and convinced that he must be joking, the young woman followed his directions to hop onto the seat of her bike. When he jumped onto his own bike and started towing her and her broken bike, she realized he was dead serious. He intended to tow her along. She remembers this encounter as "one of the most touching moments of my life" as she describes the scene of the man "vigorously pedaling and dripping sweat as he towed the American princess through the barren desert."

Villagers they saw along the way called out "Good morning!"—"*Ney Yibeogo!*" "After a while," she says, "I began to feel terribly guilty, posed on my bike, waving like a Rose Parade float queen."

Up and down the hills they proceeded, the man pushing the pedals of his bike, sweating profusely on the way up and leaning back and waving as she passed him on the way down, "like two horses on a carousel, rotating positions, each time with more laughter and amazement at our plight."

Two hours later, they arrived at her destination. "He was exhausted, I was giddy and in awe of his generosity. I took a long look at his face and those kind eyes, and I told myself never to forget it, because this man is the heart of Burkina Faso. This man is not an exception in his culture. He is the very essence of it."

She says:

> When I think back on the moment when I was stranded on the deserted cow path, there was a part of me that was calm, because I knew where I was. I was in a place where you never feel alone or abandoned because someone will always come along to help you; where a starving woman would give her last bowl of food to a stranger; where kids are elated to play with an old tire and a stick. . . . These principles are more than just cultural values, they are a way of life. . . . Burkina Faso means "the

land of upright and courageous people." It is one
of the poorest countries in the world, but a place
where I learned what giving truly means.[2]

A little man on a dusty road in Africa responds with an
open heart to a stranded stranger on the side of the road.
She is deeply influenced and shares the story with readers
around the world. Now as you read this story in this book,
what effect will his action have on you? One act of generosity, no matter how small, generates yet another. The flow of
giving and receiving is endless.

TEN

I Take Up the Way of Engaging in Sexual Intimacy Respectfully and with an Open Heart

In order to know the Way in perfect clarity, there is
one essential point you must penetrate and not avoid:
the red thread [of passion] between our legs that cannot be severed. Few face the problem, and it is not
at all easy to settle. Attack it directly without hesitation or retreat, for how else can liberation come?
—Sung-yuan Yu-Lu, *Dainihon Zoku Zokyo*[1]

If there is anything that can broadside our thoughts and
emotions, it's sexual desire. What begins as a biochemical
resonance that drives all of life quickly winds its way through
the labyrinth of sensations, desires, fantasies, and wishes
that can lead us into deep intimacy or into escapism or even
into brutal abuse of others. But as the twelfth-century Zen

master quoted above reminds us, if we have any hope of taking action with clarity and freedom, then we must face directly the passion we cannot sever.

Sex is one of the most powerful energies we can experience as human beings and the one that perhaps we experience the most confusion about, so it is not surprising that cautions around sexual behavior have been stressed for anyone who hopes to cultivate a clear mind. In a monastic environment, this precept is often worded so as to encourage celibacy, Do Not Engage in Sexual Activity, but for the lay practitioner it is often worded, Do Not Misuse Sex, or Do Not Misuse Sexuality. The heat of sexual desire and the power of its energy, however, will not dampen so easily. Even attempts to pigeonhole it into right, wrong, good, bad, moral, immoral are, at best, limited restraints. It won't be ignored. So I take this precept not so much as a restraint around sexuality, but as an invitation to know it intimately. A student says it this way:

> I take up the way of stepping into sexual intimacy
> not only naked in body, but in heart. And I take up
> the way of meeting the craving, as well as the fear
> of the craving; the desire for closeness as well as the
> fear of closeness; the greed for power as well as
> the fear of power; the escape as well as the union.

Sex is the behavior most laden with all types of social, cultural, and religious beliefs, especially taboos about appropriate intimacy (with whom, when, what kind, and so forth).

There is no doubt that engaging in sexual energy out of greed, manipulation, anger, or power can result in suffering that ripples much further than the immediate people involved. There is also no doubt that engaging in sexual energy with honesty, sensitivity, and an open and giving heart can be a vehicle for deep intimacy. The power and usefulness of working with this precept, however, is not in simply trying to determine correct behavior or valid taboos, but in inquiring deeply into the ways we use this powerful energy, which has the capacity to break down all barriers, to solidify and reinforce our individual safety zones.

The key to unlocking the teaching here is in exploring what it might mean to *misuse* sexual intimacy, something that is so natural in our lives. This might be easier said than done. If we are sexually active, the very surge and power of the energy can make it difficult to slow down and observe. On the other hand, if we are sexually inactive, we may think that this precept doesn't even pertain to us. But we do not have to be involved with the physical act of sex for it to play a powerful role in our interaction with others.

Recently someone asked me if I thought people are more obsessed with sex today than they were, say, two thousand years ago. Certainly, sexual references are harder to escape nowadays, whether in advertising, television, movies, literature, or music. Consequently, it may seem that unless we are engaged sexually, we aren't successful in our lives. And even when our bodies want to turn naturally toward aging and diminishing sexual desire, we may get the message that we're supposed to prolong our sexual activity. But I wonder if individuals really are more obsessed inwardly now than they were two thousand years ago. The subject of sex is abundant in ancient texts, including the Bible. Maybe what we are witnessing today as sexuality becomes more and more open is a questioning of constraints and even double standards that have dominated our culture in the past. Today we are open to discussions about the suffering caused by rape, incest, sexual abuse, and harassment. We are also learning as a society to acknowledge the deep love and intimacy that can take place between nonheterosexual partners. Whether our society's interest in sexuality is a growing cultural obsession or simply increased sexual openness is a subject for another discussion.

The Red Thread

So what is this "red thread" of passion? Is it simply a biological drive for the propagation of the species? The poet Ralph Waldo Emerson writes:

> The preservation of the species was a point of such necessity that Nature has secured it at all hazards by immensely overloading the passion, at the risk of perpetual crime and disorder.[2]

Sexual desire is most certainly a biological drive. Scientists are able to determine that sexual passion is located in an ancient structure of the brain called the hypothalamus. The hypothalamus regulates temperature, thirst, hunger, and sexual drive, as well as other functions that contribute to the body's basic workings for survival. However, the purpose of this desire, and the reason for its place among our most basic neural survival structures, is a different issue. If we were to speak to a biologist, sexual desire would most likely be attributed solely to the preservation of the species. The rest of the hypothalamus contributes to the survival of the individual organism, so sexual drive is attributed to the survival of our species, both in terms of generational progression as well as the benefits of genetic recombination through sexual reproduction.

However, might there be other reasons for sexual desire to be a basic drive? For example, could human passion act as the agent for our ability to experience our deepest connections to one another, allowing for the power of intimacy between beings? When we begin to explore what bars us from this intimacy, we begin to engage our sexuality with respect and an open heart. Author John Cheever expresses it this way:

> If my hands tremble with desire they tremble likewise when I reach for the chalice on Sunday, and if lust makes me run and caper it is no stronger a force than that which brings me to my knees to say thanksgiving and litanies. What can this capricious skin be but a blessing.[3]

True intimacy means standing openly with ourselves and others. Misusing intimacy, especially sexual intimacy, relates to the ways we may separate ourselves from others, thus avoiding being absolutely present. It can show us how even in the deepest clutches of a physical embrace, we can be distant and disconnected. This precept can help us understand this perceived separation very deeply by revealing ingrained patterns of thinking and feeling related to sexual intimacy. For example, we may involve ourselves in superficial multiple relationships or move from one partner to another as a way to use sex as an escape from feelings of being alone and unwanted. We may use it as a distraction to avoid or numb feelings, never coming to really know what it is we're trying to escape. Sometimes we may use it to shut off or short-circuit thoughts, to detour around the endless cycle of obsessive thinking, never knowing intimately what fuels the escape into our head. We might become greedy for the sexual high, the surge of heat that wipes out feelings of isolation, loneliness, unworthiness, and so on.

The greed may not be limited simply to our immediate release of tension, the gratification of the urge, but may also
include greed for feeling loved, needed, important, and powerful, and give rise to anger and jealousy.

One of the most common misuses of sexual intimacy arises
out of loneliness. The heart is indeed a lonely hunter, and
loneliness is one of the underlying emotions that can mani-
fest in several ways around sexual attachments. It can take
the form of avoidance: purposefully not engaging in any
sort of sexual intimacy for fear of rejection, or in order to
perpetuate feelings of worthlessness. Promiscuity or being
involved in a sexual relationship with multiple partners
may be another attempt to ensure connection, to construct
or forge an imagined relief from loneliness and the sadness
that often accompanies it. When we are lonely, we often
experience a deep sadness and perhaps even depression. We
desperately hunger for intimacy and long to be chosen as an
important object in someone else's life.

Years ago when I was a young single mother with three
beautiful children and supportive parents, I often felt very
lonely, especially around the holiday season. I used to wonder, why are my children and my loving family not enough?
Why do I feel so alone and so deeply saddened? We've all
heard the refrain about the loneliest person in the biggest
crowd. What I came to realize over time was that feeling
alone had nothing to do with other people. The loneliness
I was experiencing came not from who or how many people
I was surrounded with, but from a deeper yearning to be
chosen. My family did not choose me. We were born into
the relationship. Lovers, however, would choose me, thus
validating me in some way.

As mentioned earlier, exploring this precept can be a
useful tool for uncovering long-held requirements and core

beliefs even if you are not sexually active. The key is to take an honest look at what is going on. Even if you have chosen a form of celibacy, depending on your particular libido, you may experience sexual energy nevertheless. The point is that you explore with openness the ways sexual desire weaves its way through the labyrinth of daily existence. Whether we choose abstinence, celibacy, or sexual engagement, we can learn something.

Frozen Passions

There's a Zen story that illustrates this point.

> There was an old woman who oversaw the lodgings and food of a spiritual hermit living high in the mountains near her cottage. Each day, she trekked up the mountain to bring him food and to see that he had what he needed to support his meditation. After many years of doing this, she decided it was time to test his understanding, so she sent her lovely young granddaughter to bring him his food. She also instructed the young woman to entice him by resting her head on his lap and to ask him, "How's this?" So, one cold, rainy morning, the girl made her way up the mountain and entered the hermit's hut. She gave him his food and then rested her head on his lap, asking "How's this?" The hermit jumped up and turned away quickly, expounding the words of a poem, "The withered tree is rooted in bitter cold. During these winter months, no heat rises, no life." He then pushed the girl out of the hut into the cold rain without even a cover.

Returning to her grandmother's cottage, the girl relayed the hermit's behavior in the hut. The old woman exclaimed, "That good-for-nothing! To think that I have supported him in his practice all these years and this is the extent of his understanding! There's not even an ounce of compassion in him!" The old woman traveled once more up the mountain and set fire to the hermit's hut, thus sending him down the mountain and into the world.

Why was the old woman so angry? Why did he fail her test? The point about this story is that the hermit, in spite of his reclusive life, had not learned that the heart of compassion and wise action lie neither in totally engaging in our passions nor in the denial of our human passions at the expense of others. Even after all those years of meditation, he still wasn't able to come out from behind his wall and be fully present in his experience. Instead, he speaks a poem about what he thinks he should feel and ignores what he truly feels. Not even the words he uses are original—his relationship to his sexuality has been entirely artificially created as he recites the poem. What's more, he uses the woman's granddaughter to prove his ability to overcome sexual desire in a prescribed fashion. This sort of practice, the wise old grandmother knows, is useless without experiencing the deep red thread of passion within our bones.

THE PRACTICE

We begin our practice with this precept by purposefully bringing awareness to the physical sensations associated with sexual energy. A good place to begin practice with this precept is in the body—to explore some of the beliefs and sensations that arise for us around sexuality. Taking your favorite comfortable position, bring your attention to the body.

Stay relaxed with a gentle focus on breathing in and out. Now bring into mind any image, sense, or word that excites you sexually. It can be a person, a picture, a smell, a melody. It can be a word or phrase. If you notice you begin to judge the object of your attention as good, bad, sick, or something else, just identify those thoughts as *judging* and return to the object of your attention. When you've activated something, you'll notice a change in your bodily experience. The breath may quicken, deepen, or shorten. The body may slightly contract or tighten. You may feel certain sensations. You may also feel nothing. Feeling nothing is also an experience. What is that numbness like? Deepen the body scan by paying closer attention to the heart, gut, and genital areas. Do some areas feel more remote than others? In other words, do you find that awareness doesn't go to certain areas? If it doesn't, try moving in that direction and see what happens. Do any thoughts, emotions, or judgments, like I can't do this or I'm not good at this, arise around this numbness? If you notice a feeling such as fear, shame, hurt, anger, or power, sub-vocalize the label and return to just breathing and feeling the sensation.

Remember, as in all inquiry, you're not demanding or measuring. You are just inviting by purposely bringing awareness to your point of inquiry. The power of this exercise is in the driving light of the question that seeks no answer. Don't necessarily expect your experience to be pleasurable or even sexual. The aim of this exercise is to bring into awareness what thoughts and beliefs you associate with sexual energy. Sexual energy may rise, but fear, anger, shame, or other emotions may rise. In fact, other emotions like anger or fear may often ride piggyback on sexual energy.

Deepening the Inquiry

Engage the Observer

Now bring your inquiry into your daily experiences, noticing what sorts of reactions different situations bring up for you. Here, you are trying to bring out into the open not only your personal experience with sexual energy, but also attitudes and judgments you may hold toward others regarding their sexuality. The intention at this point is to be observant as much as possible to what goes on in you on the street, in the bus, at work, wherever you see or interact with others. Do certain types of people turn you off or on? Do you find yourself judging and closing off to certain individuals? Give yourself permission to feel and think without being restricted. Be open and observe whatever thoughts or feelings may arise. Do you notice any patterns? As in the exercise above, keep your inquiry at the level of invitation. You are not demanding anything to reveal itself. You are simply removing the veils covering your deepest holdings of the self-centered dream.

You may do this exercise for days, weeks, or even months before you notice anything consciously. But if you are gentle and patient with yourself, over time you will begin to open the door, Enter Here, and find your deepest associations with sexual energy—how you experience it yourself and how you view others. Once we are able to do this, we can really begin to do the further work of exploring the ways in which we may use this energy to reinforce our patterns of self-identity that can cloud *what is*.

We might think of our relationship to sex as located somewhere between two bookends. On the one end is the engagement in pure, wondrous sexual energy and communion—nothing to grasp, nothing to attach. On the other extreme are behaviors that can be alienating and destructive.

We discover how to live this precept by exploring how we spin out the fantasy of a separate self by using sexual intimacy. It is useful to explore deeper into the underlying body and thought reactionary patterns. In other words, as with the other precepts, we need to begin to study who we think we are. This practice can uncover the basic beliefs about our identity that can fuel and direct our actions fueled by sexual energy. Even if you are involved in what you consider a happy, well-balanced sexual relationship, you may find it useful to explore this practice. Remember that the purpose of precept practice is not to fix ourselves, but to find real freedom to engage in life, realizing clearly that all that we think we are, all that we believe we must have, and all that we strive for is only an illusion, part of the self-centered dream. Each and every one of us can know this, if we are willing to stumble around in the muddy water of our desires and discover the clarity of an open heart.

Exposing Beliefs

In the previous exercise, we awakened the observer to stop, look, and listen to what takes place in the mind and body in the presence of sexual stimulus. Now we deepen the inquiry by shedding light on how our attitudes about sex can be used to reveal deeply held beliefs that may fuel the actions we take to fulfill a deeper lust for self-gratification. What sorts of thought/emotion patterns did you notice? Did you tend to connect sensuality with a specific thought or emotion—closeness, power, love, safety? You may find that you have more than one association. Choose one association and go through the following questions:

1. When I connect sexual energy with _____, what am I creating?

2. When I connect sexual energy with _____, what am I not creating?

3. When I connect sexual energy with _____, what gets resisted? Does this resistance resonate within my body?

Turn and explore by scanning the body to bring awareness to how the body speaks. Remember, the key is inviting, not demanding. Awareness used in this way does not *look* for sensation, it just gently turns the light beam of attention toward the body and breathes in and out and observes what may show up. If you notice a sensation, pause and allow yourself to feel the sensation, breathing in and out, allowing the energy to ebb and flow and be open. If you experience numbness, then rest in the presence of that experience.

4. If I separate sexual energy from _____, what, if anything, occurs? What, if anything, gets resisted?[4]

Student Response:

1. When I connect sexual energy with love, closeness gets created.

2. When I connect sexual energy with love, other ways of experiencing love are not created.

3. When I connect sexual energy with love, I resist other ways to experience love.

4. Nothing seems to get resisted. I just feel open.

The above questions and responses are only examples. Beliefs we hold around sexual energy are numerous: fragility, hostility, impotency, contempt, power, and safeness are all ideas that are bound up in our perceptions of sexual intimacy. When we allow these beliefs to enter into and cloud our understanding of intimacy, to get in the way of an open experience of sexuality as a pure, strong connection between individuals, we have misused our sexual energy.

CONVERSATIONS

Student: So it seems what determines what is *misusing* sex is how our actions engage us in cutting off from what we want to avoid in ourselves. And it doesn't matter if we do that alone or with other others.

Diane: Exactly. Any time we use sexual energy to escape or to alter our experience, our present mind state, we are putting up a wall to *life as it is.* We perceive ourselves as separate and are driving ourselves further from the mark and deeper into desire and grasping. This is what I would call *misusing.*

Student: But isn't what you're calling sexual energy simply a lot of substances being released by the brain? How do we get from that basic biochemical fact to it becoming a way in which we support the ego identity—something that can be misused and not just chemically transmitted?

Diane: Indeed, erotic feelings and thoughts carry with them very potent chemicals. Sometimes we associate these feeling with intimacy and love and become addicted to them, especially if we have experienced short-term satisfaction and relief from some of the ways we misuse sexual intimacy, as I mentioned earlier.

Student: Can you say something about promiscuity as a misuse of intimacy?

Diane: Beyond the initial infatuation, a sexual attraction at a deeper level of closeness can be threatening because we sense we are being revealed. This can be scary, so we might look around for new sexual partners. Depth of intimacy is replaced with breadth of sexual encounters. This can be tricky, especially in open relationships where two or more parties agree that it's okay to be involved with multiple partners. I am not making a statement here for or against such arrangements, but I am making a very strong suggestion that that is easier agreed to than done. I would advise anyone in that sort of setup to look very, very closely at the level of intimacy they are allowing to develop in any of the relationships and to be very vigilant as to emotions such as jealousy, feeling left out, and so forth, that they may be repressing for the sake of a perceived freedom. I would also ask the question: What comes up for me when I think about committing to just one person?

Student: Despite this discussion of loneliness, need for acceptance, and wariness of deep intimacy, I'm still not clear about how sex and fear relate.

Diane: If we have a core belief that if we reveal ourselves, something dreadful will happen, then we are fearful of closeness, and so we may avoid sexual engagement altogether or we may keep it pretty superficial by having multiple partners or keeping it short term and not committing. For example, we may have the core belief that we are fundamentally flawed and therefore unlovable. Sexual encounters can threaten to blow our cover, so that those *flawed* and *unlovable* buttons get pushed, and we are catapulted into the experience of that core belief. We feel fearful and vulnerable. So in order to avoid this experience, we may hold very rigidly the limits of our sexual engagements. Or, on the other hand, we may try to keep our involvement safe by having backups of several partners.

If we are practicing with this precept, when fear and/or vulnerability arise, we should turn toward the experience of Just This and allow its energy to flow openly, witnessing the ebb and flow of its power. We observe the thoughts and emotions surrounding the physical experience, and over time we watch them lose their power. But in order to do this last part of the practice, we must first be willing to really face head-on what our relationship is to sex. This is the way we take up the precept of *engaging in sexual intimacy respectfully and with an open heart.*

ELEVEN

I Take Up the Way of Letting Go of Anger

> Anger no longer seems a lunatic stranger locked in
> the basement, but a familiar shadowy twin who sud-
> denly appears in the room in unexpected guises. I
> now recognize anger as a frequent visitor in my life.
>
> —A Student's Rendition of the Vow

What follows in the next few pages of this book is not going
to teach you how to wipe anger out of your life. What it will
offer is some helpful ways for you to wake up to your particular relationship to anger, whether you confront it in
yourself or in others. This is the key—to learn how to be
awake in the presence of anger instead of swinging into
blind action. When, if only for a moment, we can turn our
attention to the sensory experience of anger, then we do
what Stephen Levine calls "taking tea by the fire . . . to take
tea with our outrage or confusion . . . to meet [it] eye to eye.
We learn about relating *to* instead of *from* anger."[1]

Letting Go of Anger

This precept is often worded Do Not Indulge in Anger, but the point of this precept is not to "stuff" or deny anger, but to come to understand anger intimately so that we may take more skillful action in its presence—to spot the difference between action that arises out of *self-centered* anger and action that arises out of *life-centered* anger, anger that is a genuine response to support life. The rippling effect of self-centered anger is endless. While I'm not suggesting that this precept invites us to fan the flames of anger, it does point us in the direction of experiencing it directly and knowing the difference between using it skillfully or unskillfully. Like anything else, we can't understand something that we do not investigate. Not hanging on to it, not pushing it away, not stuffing it, we can learn how to quickly identify the patterns of our thinking and the body's reactions that rise when it comes. Anger, like any other human emotion, is a natural occurrence. It is possible to experience its power and force without being destroyed or caught by it. Its nature is like a flame that burns bright and clear, then disappears. To practice this precept, to let go of anger, is to come to know its workings in and through us and experience its energy in our lives. This is the way of *letting go of anger.*

> Someone whispered to a man one late afternoon that his wife was making a fool of him by secretly meeting her lover in the garden every night. Being prone to quick temper, this fellow grew furious, vowing to catch her and her lover in action. So when darkness came, he climbed high into a tree in the rear of the garden and waited for them to appear. He waited into the night, and as he grew cold and tired, the anger grew stronger and stronger. But no one appeared except for a raccoon and a stray

cat. Perched high in the tree, the man grew increasingly furious, thinking of all the scenarios that were taking place behind his back. In fact, he grew so upset that he fell right out of the tree. He lay on the ground cursing and threatening and making such a ruckus that his neighbors ran out of their houses to investigate the commotion. By this time, worked into a frenzy, this silly fellow blurted out to everyone that he had been hiding in the tree for several nights waiting to catch his unfaithful wife and her lover. Then one of the neighbors stepped forward, scratched his head, gave the man sprawled on the ground a quizzical look, and blurted out, "But you're not married!"

As we can see from this story, anger can dupe us into chasing all types of shadows. But anger can also inform us, alerting us to conditions and situations for which we should take action. How can we meet anger, and what can we learn from it? This question is what this precept is about.

Anger is a tricky emotion for many of us. We may hold the belief that anger in any situation is wrong, unacceptable, unspiritual, dangerous, or should be squelched at its earliest signal. Some of us wear it like an armband signaling to others, "Don't mess with me." Others hide it like that lunatic stranger in the closet. For some it's like a landmine waiting to be tripped by any unfortunate passerby. For others, it supplies a sense of power and strength. Some wonder, What's all the fuss? Who, me? Angry? And for some of us, being in the presence of others' anger frightens and cowers us into the mind and body's secret silence. As we begin working with this precept, it's useful to first explore some of the beliefs we have about anger.

CONVERSATIONS

Student: My strongest belief about anger is that I shouldn't have it.

Diane: Why?

Student: It makes me appear out of control.

Diane: So your thought is, Anger makes me appear out of control. Any other beliefs about anger?

Student: Anger kills.

Diane: Anger kills. Any others?

Student: It's good to get rid of your anger.

Diane: But what is your belief about anger? Why is it good to get rid of it?

Student: Because when it is not expressed, it erodes the insides.

Diane: Erodes the insides. The belief, then, is that it's destructive in some way?

Student: Yes. The belief is anger is always destructive.

Another Student: If I were a better person, I would have a better way of dealing with this situation than being angry about it.

Diane: So what's wrong with anger? What's the belief?

Student: It's a sign that there is something else wrong, that I have bad coping skills or something. Then anger shows I'm a failure. I should be able to detect anger more quickly, before I get the sensation of a lot of anger.

Diane: From within this pattern of thinking, why is it important to catch the anger early?

Student: Because it is not a good thing to have.

Diane: True. But from within the self-centered thinking, why not?

Student: Because I have the belief that anger is bad. Anger *is* powerful. But I guess I'm not sure that anger is *always* bad; it can also be protective. I feel it's okay for me to express anger about laws that are unjust to other people. That energy of anger is okay—but when it comes to standing up for myself, it's not okay.

Diane: Why is it not okay? In other words, what is the belief *about* anger? Is it destructive? Is it hurtful?

Student: It can be.

Diane: If the belief is that anger can hurt people, are you included in that hurt?

Student: What I'm really afraid of is that it will show my weakness.

Diane: It will show weakness. Yes. This is the belief we've been circling around as it comes into the light—anger will reveal my weakness.

My Anger

Anger can rise out of a stack of dirty dishes our housemate leaves in the sink, the homework our kids forgot to complete, or bombings and useless slaughters of innocents seen on the news. It can be directed outward, inward, or have no direction at all. It can be simmering, boiling over, felt, or numbed. Its faces are many and its force can strengthen or destroy. Its mask of power covers fear and powerlessness. It seems to have a power of its own, appearing as little moments of madness when reason and logic fall away. We may try to avoid it, ignore it, hang on to it. We may identify it as *yours* or *mine*.

> Once a student asked the teacher, "Please, can you help me rid myself of my anger?"
>
> The teacher responded, "I can help you get rid of your anger, but first you need to show it to me."
>
> The student protested, "But I'm not angry at this moment. I can't show it to you." So the teacher sent the student away, instructing him to find his anger and bring it back to show the teacher.
>
> "After you do this," she said, "I can help you."
>
> When the student returned, he reported to the teacher, "I looked everywhere but could not find my anger."
>
> The teacher answered, "Glad I could be of help!"

The student in the story has identified himself as an *angry person,* but when those habits of mind and body are not enticed, he cannot find the anger. We might think of each rising of anger as dots on a page appearing so close together they give the impression of a solid line. But in reality, what this student is identifying as *his* anger are multiple reactions triggering chemical, biological, and psychological occurrences in his mind and body. These events arise and fall away moment by moment. But unless we've done some observation of anger, we're not likely to experience it as a fleeting, momentary event. Blindly spinning in the thoughts and bodily sensations of the anger state is what could be called *indulging in anger.*

Whether it's simmering frustration, sputtering confusion, or boiling rage, it's very difficult to turn on the light beam of awareness to stop-look-listen. As with sexual energy, it can be very difficult to *find* its dead spot, let alone *rest* in it. Aspirations to open to it and invite it in so that we can get to know it more intimately can only be, at most, strong encouragement. But if we are clear in our intention to come to know where we stand in anger, then something, over time, begins to change. We may find, sometimes in retrospect, that we do not so quickly react from or to the heat of the fire. We learn that we can grow closer, without being scorched, or by pretending there is no fire. Over time as we invite this guest into our awareness, we more often understand with each new situation and new set of conditions, each new rising of anger, the difference between reacting and responding to its powerful energy as it passes through us.

Life-Centered and Self-Centered Angers

When people first take up the way of this precept, the concern about when anger is okay and when it's not always seems to present a conundrum. I think most of us would like a tidy list of appropriate angers and inappropriate angers, but when are the emotions of life's situations ever that simple?

The key is to really know whether the anger motivates actions that benefit the well-being of ourselves or others, or if it motivates actions that are hurtful to ourselves or others. One action we can say is life-centered; the other action we can call self-indulgent. Life-centered anger has the power to be open and transformative. It can serve as a wake-up call. It rises and falls quickly and is never held onto.

Here I would like to offer a clear example of the transformative power of anger. Enraged when her thirteen-year-old daughter was killed by a drunk driver, who had a record of repeated drunk driving offenses but was still carrying a valid California driver's license, Candace Lightner cofounded MADD—Mothers Against Drunk Drivers. Its mission is to stop drunk driving, support victims of this violent crime, and prevent underage drinking. Spurred into action by the rage and pain of their experiences, members of MADD have engaged in activism that has resulted in the passage of federal and state anti-drunk-driving laws and has contributed to saving many lives.

Life-centered anger is filled with potential for useful action. It grows in intensity as we indulge our thinking and action from within it. Its price is a closed heart and mind.

The Power of Life-Serving Anger

Once there was a samurai who wanted to master the realms of heaven and hell. So he made his way to an old and frail monk who lived high in the mountains and who was renowned for his great understanding. Reaching the hut tired and cold, the samurai barged his way through the door without even knocking and demanded a place by the fire and something warm to eat. Startled, the monk, who had been sitting by the fire sipping tea, quietly put down his teacup and went to fetch some warm food for the samurai. After he had eaten and calmed down a bit, the samurai turned to the old monk and in a gruff voice demanded, "Show me the way to master heaven and hell!"

WAKING UP TO WHAT YOU DO

The old monk again put down his teacup and stood up, barely reaching the samurai's shoulders. He looked the samurai in the eye and let out a harangue: "What gives you the idea that I'd teach you anything? You're nothing but a dumb fool. Your breath stinks and your teeth are rotten. You look like you haven't bathed in months and your speech is vulgar and foolish."

The samurai's eyes bulged and his face grew red with fury. He raised his sword above the old monk's head as if to strike him. His breathing was hard, and he looked as if he would burst. Directly under the shadow of the samurai's sword, the monk sat down, picked up his teacup, took a sip, and said, "That's hell."

Dumbfounded and deeply moved by the old monk's willingness to risk his life to teach him the meaning of hell so profoundly, the samurai lowered his sword. His heart filled with appreciation and love for the generosity and open heart of this fearless monk. Seeing the samurai's response, the old monk continued, "And this is heaven."

Here is a clear example of the difference between life-centered and self-centered anger. Hearing the old monk's harangue, the samurai fell into rage, nearly killing him. He reacted only to the insults this old man was hurling toward him. The old man, on the other hand, turned anger into a useful action. Some may take this story to illustrate how enlightened the old man was that he didn't become angry even when this boorish fellow barged his way into his hut, but I like to take a little liberty with this story and think of the old monk as a little more like me or you. Maybe he *did* experience anger when the samurai barged into his hut, but because he had learned how to stop, look and listen in the presence of this powerful emotion, he was able to let it pass through him before he opened his mouth, and thus he only feigned outrage in order to help the samurai.

When anger's energy is life centered, it can alert us to situations that go against our deepest sense of what serves life—our lives, the lives of others. When she was seventy-five years old, my teacher Jōko Beck used to take daily walks along the beach in San Diego. One day as she was walking along, she came upon two young men fighting. One was brutally beating on the other. Jōko describes how she felt an immediate surge of heat as anger rushed forth. She marched up to the young men and with every ounce of strength she had, she pushed them apart, yelling at them to "STOP IT!" Shocked to see this elderly, white-haired woman demanding them to stop hurting each other, they dropped their arms and walked away from each other. The quickening heat, the rush of adrenaline signals us to pay attention—*now!* And when we do pay attention, the open, free flame transforms into a powerful energy that ignites skillful action that responds to circumstances as they truly present themselves in the present time.

Anger can also be a signal that alerts us to how we may be mistreated. It can shine the light beam on unacceptable, abusive situations. It can be a gift, a wake-up call that triggers us to remove ourselves from the situation. But many people who have covered or ignored their anger may not experience anger at all; and by blaming themselves or having some other misconceived notion, they may remain in abusive situations. The following battered wife's account describes this type of experience:

> It's been a long haul for me to finally feel some anger about the years of abuse I took from my

husband. I was so paralyzed with fear that I couldn't get out of the situation. I felt helpless and vulnerable. Anger would have been my ally because it would have gotten me on my feet and out the door. It would have been the signal, loud and clear: "Wait a minute. No one has a right to hurt you. No one has a right to treat you that way." Sometimes I hear people say that women choose to stay in abusive relationships because it gives them something they need. I'm not so sure it's so simple. Somewhere wrapped up in helplessness and vulnerability was a core belief that I was wrong—that somehow I deserved this treatment. Anger never even flickered a spark. I wish it had. Maybe I wouldn't have waited until I feared for the life of my children and myself before I finally got out. Maybe my children would be less scarred by all the screaming and violence. But even then, I walked out the door out of fear, not anger. It wasn't until years later, and lots of practice recognizing and allowing anger to come into my experience, that I can honestly say that I believe no one has a right to hurt me, and really believe it! One day someone pushed me very roughly. I could feel the power of anger rising from the bottom of my being. What this other person was doing to me was not okay! I responded clearly and strongly, standing my ground not out of fear but out of self-respect. I said, "Take your hands off me!" and I knew I was right. Anger felt clean and real, and I was thankful that I was open to its warning. I realized I could be open to it, listen to it, and take action without clinging to it.

Self-Indulgent Anger

When we measure our well-being by the extent to which we maintain our requirements about the way we need to be or the world needs to be, then we are likely to be disappointed. And when we or the world fails to meet our requirements, then there's a good chance we'll react out of anger. What makes anger self-indulgent is the fact that we use it, *and hold on to it,* to maintain our identity or dream of self.

One way to look at the story about the man in the tree is that his self-centered dream was maintained by the belief that he had to keep constant vigilance so that he would not be duped. His angry reaction over a phantom didn't occur out of nothing. The power of the story lies in the fact that the man was so driven by his requirement to *not be taken advantage of* that he saw danger where there wasn't any.

Oftentimes, when one of my students describes a reaction of anger, I ask him, "Is there a requirement not being met here? If so, what is it? How is it? How do you think it should be?" Keeping in mind that we can so often be caught in our habitual reactionary swings, these questions can turn our awareness to the fact that we are in the middle of the swinging, something we often don't realize in the heat of anger. Bringing our awareness into the open in this way is the necessary next step if we want to open to whatever deeper core beliefs lie under our reactions.

Self-indulgence in anger can also occur as denial. Some of us get the message early on in life that anger in others and ourselves is unacceptable. And if we don't get it early on, we may pick it up later. Many of the religious *isms,* including Buddhism, can be practiced in such a way as to suggest that if we experience anger, we are not *enlightened.*

We can push the experience of anger away in any number of ways, avoiding confrontation at any cost. Sometimes we don't even realize that that's what we're doing. We may cower in the face of another's anger or measure out our involvement in the world by obsessively planning out our lives, picking the right partner, working at the right job, etc. Not that it is wrong to plan our lives and so forth, but if we engage in this sort of activity as a way to avoid feelings we are afraid to face, like anger, then we create a form of self-imprisonment.

We learn lots of ways to push anger away. Perhaps we make light and joke every time the first signal of anger arises. Or maybe we keep an expressionless face with our mouth shut whenever we disagree with someone else. Practice encourages us to identify these strategies as such, for energy as strong as anger will not be silenced. The more we try to deny it, the more likely dishonesty, either to ourselves or others, will enter into the situation.

Sometimes, this precept is taken as a prohibition against all anger, pointing to the hurtful results of its indulgence. But I think if we keep in mind that our aspiration is to respond rather than react to conditions and situations, then we can approach this precept not as a prohibition against all anger, but as an invitation to explore the difference between anger that springs out of old patterns of thinking and perceiving—a reaction—and anger that springs out as a clear indication of conditions or situations that do not serve life—a response.

THE PRACTICE

As with the other precepts, the first step in practicing with habitual patterns of mind and body is to allow an open inquiry into their workings. We engage the precept as a lighthouse beacon that lights the way along a rocky shore, so we must explore anger events in all their forms, whether it's a simmering upset or a full-blown harangue. We slowly learn to face it and embrace it. We come to know its face intimately. Invite it in and call it by its true name. This can seem very frightening. What would happen if we were to allow even a moment of presence with it? It is difficult to do when we are in the heat of it. So it's important for us to first discover where we stand with anger.

If we have had particularly strong experiences with anger, we may fear that even the slightest opening into its experience will be uncontrollable or unbearable. Perhaps we may fear that it will unleash an uncontrollable destructive energy. This is natural, so we move slowly. If we are willing to put aside our reactive actions for just one moment so that we can rest for a moment in the dead spot, listening and feeling its rhythms in our body and in our thoughts, we may discover that we've tapped an important source for transformation.

Deepening the Inquiry

Engage the Observer

Become curious about what triggers your anger as you go about your daily activities. What events set anger into motion for you? Someone cuts you off on the freeway. There's a moment of madness and you make a rude gesture. You know there's nothing positive or helpful about your reaction, but you get some sense of satisfaction—momentarily. It'll take a while, but if you have the intention to be open and observant, you'll begin to pick up on what thoughts are present when the energy rises. At first, in all likelihood, several things will happen. First, you won't remember to turn the mind toward the inquiry until after the event. Then, you will judge it—I shouldn't be thinking that way, or I did it again, or I'll never get over this. You may also find that the thoughts develop into a story about who did what, and so forth. If this happens, when you finally notice you've been off into a story (which can take seconds, minutes, or hours), just make a mental note of the thought by repeating it—"having a thought that . . ." By keeping the intention to not try to solve anything but to allow awareness of what type of thinking triggers anger reactions, you will begin to experience a little space in which your awareness can deepen so that your experience resonates and speaks. Your particular pattern of thinking and feeling around anger will emerge. Be patient. You can't recognize years of collected requirements in just a few exercises.

One person I know who worked in the post office was practicing observing his angry reactions when people criticized him. At first he tried to stop, look and listen to all of his angry uprisings at work, but found it impossible because they were so frequent. So instead, he decided to just focus on interactions with people who bought stamps. Every time a person ordered a stamp, that was the signal for him to pay attention. If he was criticized in the encounter, he hit the jackpot. If not, he would just move on to the next person. Over time, what was interesting was that by not imposing an impossible task on himself, he naturally began to observe his reactions to criticism with people who ordered Priority Mail or had complaints about their delivery. Once we engage the observer and the beacon light of attention lights up our object, it begins to spread wide.

Enter into the Dead Spot

Once you more frequently notice your reactions, it is important to *allow* their presence in open awareness, so if judgmental thoughts arise, you can just repeat them to yourself and move on: Having a thought that I'm still getting angry over. . . . Or, I don't feel anything and I should. What begins to emerge over time is an understanding of the ways in which we indulge in anger. Sometimes people will say that they know they are angry but don't have a feeling in their body. Be patient. It takes time sometimes for the mind to connect the thoughts with the body, especially if our style is to spin in our thoughts. There are many practices to help us make that connection, and working with a teacher can help us in this way. Sometimes just ask yourself, other than my thoughts, what other signals are there that I am angry? Don't demand an answer. The question is an invitation to feel, and for some of us, this is new and frightening. Just opening, inviting, what naturally wants to reveal itself will come to the surface in time. You may begin to notice that tightening in certain areas of the body or breath holding is subtly associated with certain emotions and thoughts, such as frustration or jealousy. Try to relax and rest in the experience of Just This. In time you will notice that whatever you experience is just a passing wave of energy. The key is to allow—don't try to change it, manipulate it, or get rid of it.

After you have been practicing with this precept for a while, you can intensify the practice by purposely putting yourself in a situation that you know will ruffle your feathers, and then work with it from there. This is a way for you to enter into the dead spot. For example, if there is a particular person or situation you often avoid because you get irritated, purposely plan to seek it out. Try having coffee with the person at work you avoid. Call someone who pushes your buttons. Again, keep it simple. It doesn't take much to push our buttons if it's the right person and the right conditions. You have created your own controlled experiment so that you can carry on with the practice of experiential inquiry, watching what grows and incubates in the situation. Don't expect miracles. There will be times when this is relatively easy and times when just staying present for a few seconds will be an enormous task.

Sometimes, we come to recognize an experience of anger that is not event oriented, but rather a subtle simmer that appears to be ever present. This experience may arise after some time with practicing with this precept. People will often experience this early in the morning when first awakening. It's hardly a whisper, but nevertheless, some slight sense of annoyance or edginess. Because there is no identified object in this sort of free-flowing experience of anger, the practice is not to try to label the thoughts but to go directly to the feeling in the body. If you notice this when you are waking up, it may be best to remain in bed for another minute or two and allow your breath to carry you in and out of the sensory experience, no matter how slight it seems. Remember, our practice is not to measure and compare the intensity of our experience from one time to another, but to meet it as it is in any moment.

As our ability to be present in the experience of what we are calling anger develops, the label of anger itself disappears and what we are left with is just a sensation of energy. At this point we no longer see it as a lunatic stranger, but rather, we have come to know it intimately as a quickening in the throat, a passing surge of heat, a heaviness in the gut—the experience can be different for each of us. Over time we find that we can be quite still and calm in the middle of the storm; we will begin to feel a sense of open space and subtle changes as the energy moves and transforms and finally is no longer something we label as anger.

CONVERSATIONS

Student: I understand what you are saying about remaining open and present to whatever the experience is, but sometimes I get so angry at my kids, I scare myself. I don't feel like I have an inch of space to experience in the middle of that heat. How would I practice with that?

Diane: Sometimes the heat of the anger is so intense that the lighthouse signals us not to look and listen but to just STOP. When I was a child and was prone to mouthing off, my father would often tell me to zipper my mouth and count to ten. Counting to ten can be an excellent practice in the heat of rage. Breathe in. Count one. Breathe out. Count two. When the mind starts to go with the thinking, wrestle it back to one, two, three. . . . Sometimes removing yourself from the situation by going for a walk or a run, locking yourself in the bathroom, taking a cool shower (or a long hot bath), is the most skillful action in the heat of rage. Try listening to your favorite music. Try dancing. Equally important as the practice of openly experiencing and inquiring into the habitual patterns of our behavior is to know when the heat gets too hot and we need out. There are times when the action that most serves life is not to take tea by the fire but to get out of the kitchen. A screaming child or two on a morning after a sleepless night can be a good time to get out of the situation quickly.

Student: I'm thinking of the violence in the news spurred by anger and hatred of one group for another. It can take the form of street gangs, a small group of kids in high school opening up fire on another group, or something as big as terrorist groups. How is the anger I might feel toward my boss or my neighbor or my kids different from this type of group anger?

Diane: Anger is anger. There's no two ways around it. For sure, if you slap your child out of anger or you curse your neighbor or boss, that is, in a sense, different in outcome from, say, opening fire in a library filled with high school students or driving an airplane into a building. But in terms of anger, there's no difference between the two. The difference is what we do with it.

Today we see a great deal of group hatred that takes the form of religious, ethnic, political, and ideological differences. What draws people together to take group action out of anger is each individual person's anger. The group may serve as a container for the individual's anger, but it does not create it. That comes from the individual. So when we witness some of the atrocities in the world that we have of late, it seems to me that what we are witnessing, in part, is what happens when an individual's fear, hopelessness, powerlessness, and so forth, get recognition within a larger group. The individual's reactions to those experiences are generalized and legitimized, at least within the group, and any hope of self-inquiry is lost.

If we were always free of our dream of who we think we are, there would be no anger, no need for a precept. But one way or another we do have moments of anger, unless we're completely free of all self-centered thinking. Intelligent practice remembers that the value of practicing with the precepts lies not in how it measures our distance along the idealized path to enlightenment, but rather how it helps us live in the everyday circumstances of our lives. In the real life of most of us, we yell at our kids, we shout back at our partner, and we get angry with our political leaders.

So the most helpful way of working with the precept is not to try to not become angry, but to watch what happens when anger arises. In the open listening of the experience, the tumultuous storm of thoughts and sensations settles as we open and allow our awareness to settle into the eye of the storm. What is revealed there are our holdings, our stubborn insistence that life follow our agenda. We see them clearly for what they are, and we take action out of that clarity.

TWELVE

I Take Up the Way of Supporting Life

> Our life on this earth is not just a random event
> among billions of other random cosmic events that
> will pass away without a trace, . . . it is an integral
> component or link, however minuscule, in the great
> and mysterious order of Being, an order in which
> everything has a place of its own, in which nothing
> that has once been done can be undone.
>
> —Václav Havel, *The Art of the Impossible*[1]

Two pieces of news struck me deeply this last week. The
first was a television news report of a suicide bomber
killing dozens of innocent men, women, and children. The
second was a story a friend told me about a young woman
who offered one of her kidneys to save the life of a perfect
stranger because she had heard about the plight of a young
mother of three who was fighting for her life. What struck
me about these reports was that they demonstrated, side

by side, two extremes of what we are capable of as human beings—the most heinous forms of violence and the most virtuous acts of compassion. The action of the suicide bomber comes out of the most extreme form of disconnection, while the action of the young woman comes out of a profound recognition of our connection with one another. One action takes life; the other supports life. Most often worded Not Killing, this precept brings us face to face with the possibility of any one of us taking action from either of these extremes. One of my students renders this precept as follows:

> *I resolve to look squarely and with an open heart*
> *at the rage, fear, and sense of separateness that feed*
> *my impulses to harm others. Remembering that my*
> *life on earth must cause the death or suffering of*
> *many fellow creatures, I resolve with gratitude to*
> *abstain from cruelty and relieve the suffering that*
> *I can.*

As with the other precepts we have explored, this wording can be useful as a stop sign, giving us the directive to stop, look, and listen to our actions. Do Not Kill counterbalanced with the aspiration *I take up the way of supporting life* lead us into the heart of working with this precept —to meet the difficult questions and decisions of supporting and taking life that face us daily.

The issues addressed by this precept range from the great to the small. It runs from pouring iodine over a cut in order to kill germs, prevent infection, and, in effect, protect life, to poisoning the earth, seas, and air, capital punishment, abortion, and euthanasia. So when we consider right action when it comes to supporting life, we can find ourselves in the middle of a giant conundrum. How do we not take life and survive? Very simply, we can't. We cannot escape the fact that to support life also means to take life, be it the tiny wiggly organisms scurrying about in the cool glass of water we gulp to quench our thirst, or the steak cut from the thigh of a cow that we eat to provide iron and protein to our bloodstream.

The idea here is not to cease taking any life at all, but to face squarely our intentions and allow ourselves to make sensible choices for each and every situation. In this way we learn how to support and embrace all life. To take up the way of supporting life is to do the best we can to be open to and to preserve life whenever possible, and to be clear and present in those times we cannot. I take this precept not as an injunction to never kill, but as a directive to become more directly aware and present to the unquestionable life force in all things and why we intentionally or unintentionally ignore it and interrupt it.

An interesting occurrence often takes place when people explore the precepts with me. When we first begin working, I ask people to look at all of the precepts and choose the one to begin with that they feel they have the most difficulty with, and leave the one they feel is least evident in their lives until last. Unless a person has had a specific experience with taking the life of another, or has a particular ambivalence about being a meat eater, most people will choose to work with this particular precept as the last one.

However, the traditional order of the precepts places the taking of life first. This does have some logic. It sets up the primary directive to not bring harm to others and creates a vow to help all beings. It places us immediately in the driver's seat when we recognize that it is impossible to never kill and yet we must take the path of not harming. How are we to solve this riddle while not falling into a slippery relativism? The solution is in an unrelenting determination to be awake and present to the full scope of our reactions, which may rise out of our fear and pain, and rest in the dead spot of the experience before we swing into action. Will this guarantee that we'll always know the right thing to do? No. There are no guarantees of anything in life. But the world would be a profoundly different place if even half of the world's population committed themselves to being attentive to the truth that they are, as former president of the Czech Republic Václav Havel describes above, a link in the great and mysterious order of Being.

All the laws in the world ultimately cannot make all the decisions for us. Yet for many of us, we do not see the subtleties so quickly. Some think, perhaps, if we haven't intentionally killed another human or are vegetarians, then killing is not such a big issue. What generally happens over time as they explore the precept, however, is that people come to know not only how quickly they're likely to swat a mosquito on their forehead or smudge an ant on the table, but also how the mind of killing plays out in larger matters like capital punishment, abortion, war, and the destruction of the environment. We begin to pick up on the subtler aspects of killing like killing time and energy.

Some years ago I served as *tenzo,* or head cook, during a meditation retreat at the Berkeley Zen Center in California. During the morning lecture our teacher, Sojun Mel Weitsman, had talked about a recent brutal massacre of hundreds of people in Africa. After the lecture I had commented how wonderful I thought it was that we could be in *sesshin* (retreat) and, even if only for a few days, be free from harming or killing other beings. Later, as I was preparing the vegetables for the next day's lunch, I asked Sojun if I could pick some Swiss chard from the garden to serve with our rice. I still remember the glint in his eye when he turned matter-of-factly toward me and without hesitation quipped, "Sure. Massacre all you need to feed everyone in the meditation hall." As is sometimes said in the Zen world when a teacher seizes the moment at exactly the right opportunity to offer a teaching, "the arrow hit the mark"! I immediately saw the self-righteous mind that so easily assigns values to this life form or that life form. The mind of massacre is the mind of killing. Certainly, the massacre of innocent people in Africa was a heinous event, and I don't mean to equate it with cutting green vegetables for a salad. But Sojun's teaching went much deeper here. He pointed to the mind of massacre itself—without object. I took his teaching as a directive—stop, look, listen. Be aware, be present, and in this way support life as you take it.

At the time I am writing these words, the United States has landed a robot on the planet Mars. The mission is to see if we can find evidence of there being (or ever having been) water or life on the planet. One of the scientists on the NASA team made a remarkable comment. He said now that we are looking for life in another world, a world with possibly a whole different and foreign host of elements, we have to rethink how we identify a life form. On the planet Earth, the critical molecules of what scientists determine as *life* are DNA, RNA, protein, carbohydrate, and fat. These molecules are made of carbon, hydrogen, oxygen, nitrogen, phosphorous, sulfur, and a few other elements. However, this formula for determining life doesn't work where these elements may not exist. So, he asked, "How are we to determine what is life?" What a wonderful question to put out there for the world to hear. What a wonderful crack up the middle of our righteous minds that so easily determine this is life; this is not life. Sojun's teaching pointed to this point. If we are to know the mind of not killing, we must first crack open our opinions and prejudices and chance the unknown.

On many fronts today, we face difficult questions around supporting life—suicide, euthanasia, abortion, cloning, capital punishment, just to name a few. However, suicide, euthanasia, and abortion are three that many of us might face. Different religions have different beliefs and attitudes about these issues, but from the perspective of how we are viewing the precepts here, what is more important than passing judgment is our willingness to be open and present to the situation.

Suicide/Euthanasia

The writer Diane Ackerman, who spent one year volunteering at a suicide prevention telephone hotline, writes the following about a person she was counseling on the telephone:

> More important, perhaps, I allowed him to be suicidal. I accepted that he might one day kill himself, that he might do it tomorrow, but that my job was to befriend him on this day, in this hour, give him comfort and concern, guide him to ways of coping if possible, but even if I couldn't do that, accept that he was headed for death sometime, somewhere. We all are. It's hard to live in the tense present with suicidal callers, and not try to peer around the corner or bolster them against some future threat, but accept the narrow corridor of the call. Befriend them in the moment. Save them in the moment. Try everything. Then let the moment go.[2]

To take up the way of supporting life places us directly in the "tense present." It is when we take action from within that moment with openness and connection that we keep this precept. Even if but just for a moment we can do this, we have supported life. And by living in the moment, as Ackerman suggests, we find the only way to truly understand what supporting life means. All we have to do is choose to enter that "narrow corridor."

Proponents for and against euthanasia and abortion argue over rights of individuals to live or die, when life begins, and when it ends. The courts are filled with cases waiting for a judge or jury of twelve to decide when it's time to pull the life support systems. Will science ever really give us the answer? Up until a century ago, an ear to the chest or a finger on the wrist was the sole way to determine living or dead. Today, sophisticated brain scans measure electrical impulses and we have a much harder time deciding when someone crosses the boundary. And how are we to determine consciousness? How do we know when a human ceases to be human? These questions are not easily answered.

Certainly this precept does not answer them. Rather it drives us exactly where we need to go if we aspire to take action with humility and acknowledge this uncertainty. It is not a comfortable place to be, without an authority to determine in black or white, this is killing; this is not.

Choices—to take life, to prolong life. Doctors have to make these decisions all the time. Family members may have to make them once or twice. But each and every time we make that choice, it can only be for this one time—this situation, this set of circumstances. Like my young nephew and his wife, who after watching their six-month-old baby struggling on life-support systems for most of his short life, decided it was time to pull the plug. Cradling his tiny, frail body in their arms, surrounded by their parents, they rocked him through his passing, their hearts filled with sorrow, making their link in the mystery of Being.

Abortion

The struggle with abortion is no easier. When does life begin? When does consciousness rise? At what trimester do we change the description—from *fetus* to *baby?* Can changing a word change the truth that life in any form, at any stage, is indeed a life force? It's a life force in the initial stage of cell division; it's a life force when the organs develop; it's a life force when it takes its first breath. When the sperm and the egg join together, is life created, or is the life force taking on yet another form? These are important and very difficult questions, ones that each of us will need to answer within our own hearts.

And we also need to include other questions. What about the mother who herself might die if she carries the child? Or the extreme difficulty some families will have supporting another child? Talking to a young woman, pregnant and with two small children in tow as she begged for money on the streets of San Francisco, I found myself thinking, Why didn't she get an abortion? What kind of life can she offer this child she's carrying, and what further heartache will another mouth to feed bring to these two toddlers she already has?

I was fifteen years old when I realized I was pregnant with my first child. It was the late 1950s and abortion carried with it the stigma of dingy back rooms and quack doctors with dirty hands. The future held only a shotgun wedding, shame, and the prospects facing a high school dropout. Bleak indeed. I think that, at that time, if I could have found any way out of that pregnancy, I would have taken it. I could go on today to say that I made the *right* decision because I now have a wonderful daughter and beautiful grandchildren, all of whom bring me great joy. But I'm not so sure it's that simple. Today these are joys, but it could have just as easily turned into heartache—a sickly, disabled child, for example. Today's joy is just today—just this moment. I cannot say that because I made the right decision over forty years ago, I have happiness today. Nor can I say that my happiness today has anything to do with the decision I made forty years ago. The value of life has nothing to do with what it gives *me*. All life has its own intrinsic value, which we may never know completely or at all. Perhaps the mind of supporting life in the case of abortion rests in our refusal to forget. Abortion is not an easy decision for most people, and terminating a pregnancy doesn't necessarily terminate our recognition of the life force of which we were a part. This is true, I have found, not only for women but also for men.

If we were to look into our moral manual in the sky, we might find neat categories, such as abortion is okay in the cases of rape, disabling illnesses, or possible maternal death, but not okay if it just interferes with the mother's and/or father's lives. But no matter how we look at it, we are taking a life in whatever form it is. It makes no difference if we call it a fetus, a baby, or anything else. The question is not to find an authority that approves or disapproves of our decision but to delve into our deepest intention and then make a decision from there. There are no guarantees it will even be all that clear, but if you do the work, leaving no stone unturned, you will have done the best you could. That is all any of us can do.

Skirting around the issue by trying to determine exactly when *life* begins is not all that helpful. What is really in question is how fully open and present we are in making our decision. Do we close down to this life force? Do we exclude our partner in the decision? Do we ignore siblings and grandparents? Do we close off our own feelings? And why? What are we protecting? Furthermore, why must we protect it? What follows is a practice that I have found useful in helping people who are considering abortion.

With pen and paper list all the reasons why you would or would not carry through with this pregnancy. Whether you're the mother or the partner, be as honest as possible, exploring without judgment your intention. For example, you may find that one of the reasons you might choose to hold on to this child is to keep your already troubled relationship intact. Quite a job for a seven-pound baby! Or, knowing the child will be born with severe handicaps, you may question your ability to care for him or if you even have a right to bring a child like that into the world only to suffer. The point of this aspect of inquiry is to bring ourselves face to face with our personal agenda without commenting on our beliefs or passing judgment on them in any way. Can facing what is wanted or unwanted in this pregnancy help us face what is *wanted* or *unwanted* in our lives?

After you have spent several days doing this, go through your list and note how many points reflect your genuine concern for the unborn life and how many are concerned with how this unborn life serves or does not serve you. This can be difficult work indeed.

Say you realize that one of the reasons you would continue with the pregnancy is that you might be able to hold onto your partner. Now the inquiry can deepen, leading us to uncover deeper concerns. Maybe we're thinking, my partner won't leave me if I have the baby. This can be an invitation to delve further. Can I know that? Is it absolutely true? Really try to prove it. Ask yourself, What is the worst thing that could happen if my partner left me? What feelings and emotions arise when you have this thought? How do they resonate in the body?

Now, direct your inquiry from intention to experience. Notice what types of feeling arise as you do this exercise. Does guilt, sadness, happiness arise? Do you feel numbness? Spend several quiet times just sitting still, breathing, and relaxing into and allowing these feelings to speak. Notice ways in which you avoid them. If you feel nothing, sit still and quiet in the fullness of being numb.

When you feel you can, allow your awareness to go to the womb. Give yourself plenty of time to do this. If you are doing this with the mother, you can rest your hand on her belly. Notice any thoughts or feelings that might arise. Close your eyes and allow yourself to be open. Don't expect anything. You most likely will find yourself in the dead spot. Remember your breath. Don't judge your feelings or lack of feelings. Remember, the purpose of these practices is to help us wake up to our experience, not to demand any particular response. Notice what thoughts arise. Just note them and go back to experiencing. Notice any body sensations, any emotions or feelings that arise. Don't hold them back. Don't judge them. You are not committed to any course of action by experiencing any of these thoughts or feelings. You are only committed to being awake in this breath, this moment.

You can do this exercise as often as you like, allowing the thoughts, emotions, and bodily sensations to just be. Fears, uncertainty, and anger all are familiar to us. Be open to all those feelings and be open also to *not* feeling. This is the gift of life and what you can learn from this experience.

War—*Over There* and *Here*

Another difficult arena to take up the way of supporting life is on the battlefield of war. Here is where we can find ourselves digging ourselves deeper and deeper into our convictions in a last-ditch effort to wiggle our way out of the paradox "going to war to save lives." One truth, however, is very clear about all war: it is always a bloodbath and innocents always suffer. This is not news. The greatest writers and artists throughout history have sent us the message: war is brutal! Yet, we have not found our way out of viewing war as a solution to our conflicts.

Some argue that it's better to go to war to take down an oppressive government so that we can save the future lives of many. Others have the firm conviction that war must never be an option. So the war in the air and on the fields of nations becomes the war between individuals in their hearts. How easy it is to make our own decision by blindly following the people who speak the loudest and with the most conviction. And it's not limited to those who support killing in war. We can be just as blind in our outrage against war. Someone recently said, "Don't make war out of peace. Don't be against war; be for peace." It's not easy to give up the old patterns of self-defense. Many of us feel safe in our political domains. If we're not careful, we can be talked into anything. How are we to keep this precept when cruel despots and tyrants threaten the annihilation of whole peoples? Do we stand by and let it happen? How are they to be stopped? And what if the threat comes to our own soil? The stakes are higher than we can ever know—"nothing that has once been done can ever be undone." How do leaders go with an open heart to war when nuclear missiles are aimed at their people? I would say, they would go with grief, as if to a funeral. And I would answer the same way if asked how a person with an open heart would kill someone who was about to hurt another person, or would raise a glass to the lips of the suffering, dying human being about to swallow the pills to end her life.

Perhaps the real enemy of peace is our stubborn insistence that *our* solution is the *only* solution to a particular conflict. As excited as I am to see the recent images from the robot on the planet Mars, I wonder if we had taken all that collective brain power, energy, money, and creativity and directed it toward finding peaceful solutions to the present conflicts in the world, then couldn't we have found another way besides war?

This precept places the responsibility directly with us, the individual. How easy it is for us to blame *them*—the enemy or the government. All of the precepts come together here in the directive *don't kill; support life.* How do we block out, or *kill,* others' points of view? How do we find ways to take natural resources that aren't ours to take? How do we lie and lash out in anger? Whether we do it in our relationships, on the job, at a peace rally, or on the battlefield, what we do as individuals will find its way into our leadership. Stopping war begins with ourselves.

THE PRACTICE

Watch yourself for a week. Watch for the ways you wage war in everyday events—a spilled glass of milk, a coworker who threatens to take the promotion you're hoping for, a store clerk who insults you. What are your weapons and how do they escalate as the perceived threat grows stronger? Does your shouting shoot down your child's explanation of how the milk spilled? Do you find ways to kill your coworker's chance for advancement or come back with a cutting comment to the insult? Maybe you will not pick up a gun or strike with a bat, but will you kill in your mind? You may be surprised how close you come. When you find yourself about to do, or already having done, battle, do the inquiry work and rest in whatever the dead spot reveals. Sit in the stillness of your experience, breathing in and out. If even for just a moment, this focused, clear attention will break the reactionary patterns of harming others.

If we aspire to living a life in which we support life, then first we must open the door when the killer in us knocks. Working with this precept openly can eventually reveal some aspects of ourselves we would rather keep hidden. Recently someone shared with me the agony of caring for an aging parent with dementia. Worn down by endless calls and emergencies, hardly being able to keep up with life's ordinary challenges of work and family, he opened his heart by acknowledging that there are indeed times when he hopes that the next call would inform him that his parent has died: "There are times when I just want him to die! I want to be free of this responsibility!" This is *it*. This is the point of entry into the precept. Open the door to the knocking, as with anger. Breathe in the presence of Just This heat, hurt, and all that is the experience of your life. This is taking up the way of supporting life.

A Battered Wife's Tale Continued

It was like a lot of other nights when he came home late and drunk, filled with rage and meanness. Another go around the kitchen—pots flying, drawers strewn about, the children running off into their rooms, fearful to make a sound. Then, finally, the moment when I can breathe again as he passes out in the bedroom just off the kitchen.

I was standing by the sink, putting away the silverware strewn about the linoleum floor, and as I began to replace the butcher knife he had come at me with, I paused. The corner of my eye caught him lying there on the bed, flat on his back, the drunken murderous rage smothered in the blackness of sleep. I held the sharp knife in my hand and thought: I could end all of it right here and now. I could easily take this knife and thrust it into his chest. He would never know what happened. There, lying as he is, he's not a threat. He cannot fight back. He could not stop me. The thoughts raced as I grasped the knife. And in that moment, standing by the kitchen table, I knew completely the mind of killing. And then just a sliver, no, not a sliver, but a hair of a thought entered my mind: What would happen to my children if I killed him now and ended up in jail? So I put the knife away and resolved that when he woke the next morning and left the house, I would take the children and leave—this time, for good. And I did.

What stopped me? What turned me from taking life to supporting life? And whose life was I supporting? There was no sudden recognition that I was about to take life and that it was wrong to kill. The moral injunction "don't kill" didn't stop me. I did not put the knife away to save even my own life. I put it away to save my children's life. *What would happen to them if their mother were put in jail for life?* Supporting life comes in many faces. I think for me, this face was just that of a mother supporting the life of her children.

The path of supporting life is not simple or easy. We learn that we cannot depend on an outside authority to determine the final choice of action in all situations. Do I kill the weeds or save the grass? Do I listen to the pleas of my suffering loved one to help her die, or do I hold back and let her writhe in pain? Do I support a war because getting rid of a despot will ultimately save lives? These and many more instances are the koans we will face as we go through life. If we truly aspire to living through and taking action from an open heart, then we must recognize that there's no owner's manual that spells out right or wrong action for each and every situation we face. Being thrown back onto our own resources can send us reeling into ambiguity and doubt. We may grasp for clear *do*'s and *don't*s and what we get instead is the directive to question, investigate, be true. This is the key that opens the door to finding the wholeness of living and supporting all life.

Over time, we can begin to understand that there's a difference between just drinking water because it's there and drinking to hydrate the body. The whole glass of water; the whole life of the unborn child and the mother and father; the whole life of the killer, the victim, and the families of the killer and victim are nothing but the wholeness of life itself—unavoidable and ever present. To know that wholeness, we have to drink the whole glass of water. We drink the innocence of the unborn child and the confusions and sorrow of the mother and father. We drink the rage of the killer, the terror of the victim, and the grief and loss of the victim's family. We drink the fallen grandeur of an ancient tree when we buy the new oak table that fits so well into our home. And what we finally come to know is that the responsibility for each and every choice lies with us squarely. In the end, what it all comes down to is simply stepping up to the plate and living.

Atomic Bombs and Land Turtles

Long after he became one of the strongest opponents of the development of the hydrogen bombs on both technical and moral grounds Robert Oppenheimer, the physicist who was director of the Los Alamos laboratory during the time it designed and built the first atomic bombs (the Manhattan Project), is said to have been walking in the woods one day with a friend. He came across a land turtle, and thinking it would make a nice surprise for his grandson back at the house, he picked it up to carry it home. But just a few meters along the path, he stopped abruptly, turned back, and placed the turtle on the ground precisely where he had picked it up. He remarked to his friend, "I have interfered with life enough for one man's lifetime."

CONVERSATIONS

Student: Working with this precept worded as an aspiration, I find the onus or responsibility more on myself to take action even with situations that I'm not directly involved in. For example, even though I myself may not be directly contributing to, say, the execution of someone on death row, I am not supporting life unless I become proactive in some way. Doing nothing, or taking the position that it doesn't concern me because I don't make the laws, doesn't cut it. The precept worded this way places the choice of appropriate action in my hands.

Diane: Precisely. Whether we're looking at gossiping about others, stealing, misusing sex, telling untruths, or any of the other precepts, the power of working with the precepts comes not just in the inquiry into self-centered patterns that drive our actions, but as well, the directive is to turn the mind toward another direction. In this way the precepts are a way to train our minds.

CONCLUSION

A Process of Transformation

Not long ago at a teacher's conference, I sat with other Buddhist teachers listening to comments about teaching Buddhism by His Holiness the Dalai Lama. He said:

> There is only one important point you must keep in your mind and let it be your guide. No matter what people call you, you are just who you are. Keep to this truth. You must ask yourself how is it you want to live your life. We live and we die, this is the truth that we can only face alone. No one can help us, not even the Buddha. So consider carefully, what prevents you from living the way you want to live your life?

This is the fundamental question that the precepts ask—What action will you take given freedom of choice? How do you choose to live your life? And what motivates you to live your life in this way?

There is no timetable for completing our work with the precepts. In fact, we never really finish working with them. Seeing clearly what goes on when we take life, measure ourselves against others, indulge in anger, withhold from others, take what isn't ours to take, and any of the other re-actionary swings on our trapeze could take minutes, days, months. But when we take that time to carry the questions of the precepts into our daily activities—on the job, at home, with everyone in every situation—bringing them up, sending out a probe of inquiry, then slowly, over time, the answers will be there right in front of us, perhaps when we least expect it. It can be difficult to question our cherished opinions about our experiences. To use one of my own ex-amples, it took quite a long time for me to realize that the anger I indulged toward my mother was a reaction to a more deeply seated requirement that I be treated a certain way. When that didn't happen, I was deeply hurt and fright-ened. Anger erupted as an armor to protect me from that pain. It was frightening to hang in the dead spot of that awareness because when I was denied the reaction of anger, I only had my deepest pain and fears to face.

We begin over and over each day, each hour, each minute. We are constantly beginning our practice with the precepts, and we are always beginners. Whenever we lose sight of that, we are lost. The starting point is our refuge. Enter Here—just this moment of openness, the truth of Just This. Just This is the gateway of transformation, when we can give over completely to our experience; it transforms into the peace and joy that comes with an open heart. It is an ongo-ing process through a lifetime because the identity continu-ally creates itself. But out of our mistakes and obsessions we can know the intricacies and limits of that creation. We can know its process and how it recreates itself over and over. Over time, we buy into it less, so we are less likely to act from self-centered thinking.

In the previous discussions, I have given many examples illustrating how people may work with any of the precepts, but it's important to keep in mind that the process is a lot messier and trickier than what some of the illustrations may suggest. People are different in so many ways that the method of working with a particular precept changes with each person. The work will not always follow the sequence described here. Above all, I do not want the reader to take what's written here as a prescription or a step-by-step way of working. Often, when we stop and begin to question our actions, what gets revealed is a chaotic mess of motivations and beliefs. But if approached with patience, honesty, and intelligence, out of that chaos can arise freedom and clarity.

As with the initial inquiry, it may take some time before we feel anything. Sometimes the experience is very strong and difficult to rest in. If so, we just go to the threshold to where we feel we can handle it. This is not an endurance test of any sort. The point is to slowly come to be able to relax in this stretch, like a dancer learns to do when she stretches and relaxes into her muscles. When I sat by the phone each morning before I made that first call to my mother, I could hardly endure five breaths—my stomach was wrenching and churning so strongly. But over time, just allowing myself to rest in wherever the threshold presented at that particular time, my relationship to that wrenching changed. What I thought was the worst thing that could happen was just that—thought. It had nothing to do with what was real.

Living through the precepts is to live with their unveiling, like a *koan*, not just for a long time but for the rest of our lives. We'll never get it *right*; but we will *get it!* This is the way to keep the precepts. It is a continued effort.

At the end of our service in our Zen center, we chant, "Unceasing change turns the wheel of life and so reality is shown in all its many forms." Our work with the precepts turns us in the wheel of life and we turn it—interdependent—not one; not two. Our work with the precepts also turns like a wheel. As the beacon light of awareness lights up our actions, we see clearly how we swing into our habitual reactions of self-centered thinking. And as the power and intelligence of that awareness does its work, we stand in witness as the thoughts, feelings, and sensations lose their form, dismantling and dissolving. We rest open and alert in the power of the dead spot. Underlying holdings and beliefs—fear in all its manifestations—slowly melt into emptiness, and we are just left with breathing in and out, the sound of the children playing in the yard, the smell of the coffee— Just This. For a time, the self-centered dream has disappeared into complete awakeness. These are the turns we make over and over as we are transformed. The transformation that we aspire to is similar to the stone in the river. The stone doesn't know that it's getting worn smooth, that its shape and contour are changing. It has no idea. It just keeps accepting the river. That river is our lives. The precepts can help us meet that flow of life. The effort to be present to life's flow in an awake, aware way, and to do whatever we need to do to keep that awareness bright and sharp, is also our responsibility.

Engaging the precepts in our lives in the most ordinary way can call us out of our hiding, but in truth, there is no real hiding place. We cannot escape what we are. Sometimes we just have a deaf ear to the calling. The precepts can be the voice that jolts us awake. At times the voice is soft and hardly audible. It's easy to ignore or drown out in the din of our stories. But if we're willing to learn how to listen, we can find the teacher in any of our actions—it calls out, "here I am!" And when for even a fraction of a second we can turn with openness and curiosity toward exploring that action, then—in a moment shorter than a snap of our fingers—we've come out of hiding and into the moment of Truth. But as my teacher Jōko Beck always points out, "easy to say for sure, but not so easily done" because the last place we want to look is where we already are.

We are all experts at hiding. So it takes coaxing and prodding, from some little voice inside us, and sometimes a voice outside. We all have that voice and it can take the form of the precept itself. It is the deep intelligence that brings about the seeking to begin with. Soft or deafening, the precepts prod and coax us to come out from behind our actions that harm and hurt and to face the truth of those actions. The precepts can accompany us to places where we don't want to go but, indeed, are going. They bring us into the heart of wisdom and compassion; taking action out of this understanding is as simple and natural as drinking a glass of water.

A Primer in Awareness Practice

What follows is meant to be a very general guideline for the person who would like to have some preliminary instruction about mindful awareness practice. If it is at all possible, however, it is advisable to receive instruction from a qualified teacher in person.

Try This

Right now, remain in the position you are in—sitting, standing, lying down. Don't change anything.

Now bring your attention to your breathing, making no attempt to change it. If it's short, observe that. If it's long, observe that. Pay attention as you take in air and breathe it out. Notice the chest rising, feel the sensations in your nostrils or mouth. Take just a minute or two to do this as you turn your awareness to your breathing. Don't complicate the exercise by trying to read into it. Just do it.

You have taken the first step toward Stop. Look. Listen.

If you do nothing more than this activity for five minutes every day, you will shortly begin to notice that your awareness sharpens and you can pick up more subtleties of your breath. The key is that you don't try to make anything special out of it. In fact, there is nothing mysterious at all about being awake and present to our breath or anything else in life. It's the most natural thing we can do as humans—being present. In fact, we can't help but be present. The point is, we aren't always awake to that fact.

During the course of events on any given day, we get sidetracked easily, and even taking five minutes to develop the skill of *stop-look-listen* is not always easy. So it is useful to take up a structured approach to developing mindful awareness.

Taking a Position

Find a quiet place and a comfortable position in a chair or on a cushion. If you cannot use either of these positions, you can lie down or stand up. Several longtime practitioners at our Zen center do their awareness meditation lying down or standing because of physical limitations. Keep the eyes open and held at a 45-degree angle. Try to stay relaxed, but not limp or slouched. This means that you will want to pay attention to your body alignment.

Settling In

After you're somewhat settled in your physical position, just watch. In all likelihood, your mind will be filled with lots of thoughts or you may notice other various sensations in the body. This is normal and is going on all the time anyway. The only difference is that right now, you're aware of it.

Often these thoughts or other sensations will send a message to the body to move. It is said that when the mind moves, the body follows. If you're having a thought like, This is boring, then the body looks for something to do. It may shift position or begin to fidget. Try to notice when this happens. The key, remember, is to take note, observe, not to try to maintain some ideal position. Waking up to *how* you are holding your body is much more important than *making* your body stay straight. It takes time for the body to learn to rest in stillness. The rush-hour traffic of the freeway doesn't always end just because our car takes the exit. Depending on our lifestyle, busy lives have a way of turning into busy minds and bodies.

Breathing

The first thing we do when we are born is take in a breath. The last thing we do when we die is let out a breath. Breathing is one of the most fundamental activities we engage in. It supports us in a way nothing or no one else can, and when we observe it, it can calm us and help us see where we are at this moment.

The average person breathes sixteen breaths per minute while awake and about six to eight while sleeping. That's roughly 960 breaths per hour or over 23,000 breaths in a twenty-four-hour period. Under stress, the number of breaths can jump to a hundred per minute; it can fall as low four or five in deep meditation. Whether we're conscious of it or not, it's always with us, and when it's not, we don't have to concern ourselves with it. We do it automatically or with control. So for the purposes of developing an awareness practice, the breath can be very useful. We can think of it as telling our mind, "Okay. You want to put your attention somewhere, so put it here on the breath."

As you are sitting still, bring your attention to the breath coming in and out. Breathe naturally. You will find that thoughts, feelings, and/or sensations arise. When they do, just note them and bring the attention back to the breath. Each time we bring the attention back to breathing, even if we do it a thousand times within a few minutes, our ability to be present deepens and our resistance to just sitting in the present moment lessens.

Scanning the Body

Now, starting at the tip of your head, slowly scan down your body with your attention from head to big toe, bringing awareness to places that you find some holding. It might be helpful to think of the light beam shining down from the top of your head and spiraling down to your feet, lighting up your awareness.

Sometimes this exercise is used as a relaxation technique. However, here we are using it not primarily as a way to relax tensions in the body, but rather as way to bring attention to the places we hold in the body and in doing so, sharpen the blade of awareness. When we engage our mind in this way, quite often holdings will relax. If so, that's quite okay. Other times, people will become aware of emotional holdings within the bodily tension. This is a natural occurrence as awareness strengthens.

Observing Our Thoughts/Emotions

Usually our thoughts spin like a self-looping tape. After sitting for just a few minutes, you may discover that your thoughts are wandering, planning, or demanding something. Thinking is not bad or even undesirable. What's important is not how many or what type of thoughts we have, but what we do with them.

At whatever point in your sitting you notice a thought, take note of its content. It doesn't matter whether it seems important or unimportant. Just label it silently. For example, if you have the thought, This is boring, then say to yourself, "Having a thought that this is boring." When you notice the mind spinning, just label it, "Having a thought the mind is spinning" or "Just Spinning."

You may begin to notice that some thoughts have more emotional content than others. This activity of the mind is sometimes called *emotion-thought*. For example, a thought such as, He treated me unfairly, may be accompanied by anger or sadness. Sometimes you may become aware of the emotion immediately and note the thought-sentence that accompanies it later. Whether you experience the thought or the emotion first is of little significance; the important point is simply to be aware of whatever is going on—how that emotion/thought expresses itself in the body.

Sensory Awareness

Emotion-thoughts always have an accompanying sensory experience, whether or not we're awake to it. After a while you will be more alert to the sensory experience accompanying these emotion-thoughts. For example, if you have a thought like the example above, He treated me unfairly, you can label the thought, "Having a thought he treated me unfairly," and then pause for a moment, just following your breath in and out, keeping the beam of awareness in the body, and with a soft query ask: Is there an emotion present? Sometimes you may feel nothing when your intellect tells you you should. Other times, you won't even have to query. In fact, you may notice a very strong emotion and not even know the thought behind it. This is often the case with anger. Everyone is different and all situations and holdings are different.

Don't be surprised if some or all of this doesn't come easily. There's no timetable and you can be sure that there is a deeper intelligence within all of us that is always working and *wants* us to wake up. The potential for the awareness we are trying to cultivate is without question within all of us. So we are not trying to *get* something; we are cultivating what is ours for the taking. In time, you will find, if even for only the briefest of moments, you can be awake and fully present to your thoughts and feelings without trying to escape or change them.

A Daily Appointment with Yourself

I usually advise my students to think of their daily meditation practice not as one more thing they need to add to their *to do* list, but as an appointment they set up to meet themselves. Your meditation is the one time of the day that all you have to do is show up. It is clearly a "come as you are" meeting. There is no *wrong* state of body or mind to sit.

This is the one time of day that you don't have to do anything at all except just sit there. No requirements. Just sit there, following your breath in the presence of whatever comes up. The important point is to persist in sitting every day, whether you feel like doing it or not. Begin by sitting five or ten minutes, then slowly work up to thirty to thirty-five minutes. Set an alarm clock and place it so that you cannot see the time. Shut off your phones and computer.

Many people find it useful to have a designated sitting spot where they can leave their cushion or chair set up. It is also helpful to sit at the same time each day, if possible. The propensity of mind and body to seek habitual patterns can be used skillfully by setting up a daily appointment with ourselves.

Extending the Awareness

My teacher, Jōko Beck, has often said that we do our thirty-minute daily sitting practice every day so that we can be awake to what we're up to for the other twenty-three and one half hours of the day. A daily sitting practice sharpens our observation skills so that over time we will begin to be able to observe our mind and body reactions more readily during the course of our daily activities. As we develop this ability to observe ourselves in action, we also find that we are able to be more present as we go about our daily activities.

NOTES

Introduction: A Sink Full of Teaching
1. I will discuss Mr. Daly and this precept further in Chapter 6.
2. Shunryu Suzuki, *Zen Mind, Beginner's Mind* (New York: Weatherhill, 1997), 47.

Chapter 1. What Are the Precepts?
1. The common terminologies are: Not Killing; Not Stealing; Not Misusing Sex; Not Lying; Not Giving or Taking Drugs; Not Discussing the Faults of Others; Not Praising Yourself While Abusing Others; Not Sparing the Dharma Assets; Not Indulging in Anger; Not Defaming the Three Treasures.

Chapter 2. The Dream of Self
1. Robert Aitken, *The Mind of Clover: Essays in Zen Buddhist Ethics* (San Francisco: North Point Press, 1984), 7.
2. Ibid., 13.
3. Ibid.
4. Dogen Zenji, "Genjo Koan," in *Moon in a Dewdrop: Writings of Zen Master Dogen*, ed. Kaz Tanahashi (San Francisco: North Point Press, 1983), 70.

Chapter 3. The Dead Spot
1. Jon Carroll, "Just Grateful for the Dead Spot," *San Francisco Chronicle*, June 1993.
2. Lao Tzu, *Tao Te Ching: A Book about the Way and the Power of the Way,* trans. Ursula Le Guin (Boston: Shambhala Publications, 1998), 20.

Notes

Part Two: The Precepts
1. John Elder, *Reading the Mountains of Home* (Cambridge: Harvard University Press, 1998), 60.

Chapter 6. I Take Up the Way of Speaking of Others with Openness and Possibility
1. T. S. Eliot, *The Cocktail Party*, I, iii (London: Faber and Faber Ltd., 1950), 72–3.
2. Henri Tajfel, "Social Categorization: Cognitions, Values and Groups," in *Stereotypes and Prejudice: Essential Readings*, ed. Charles Stangor (Philadelphia: Psychology Press, 2000), 49–63, xii.
3. James Baldwin, *Price of the Ticket* (New York: St. Martins, 1985).
4. Aitken, *Mind of Clover*, 69

Chapter 7. I Take Up the Way of Meeting Others on Equal Ground
1. Dag Hammarksjöld, *Markings* (New York: Ballantine, 1964), 151.
2. Rainer Maria Rilke, "At once the wingèd energy of delight," in *The Selected Poetry of Rainer Maria Rilke*, ed. and trans. Stephen Mitchell (New York: Random House, 1982), 261.

Chapter 8. I Take Up the Way of Cultivating a Clear Mind
1. Barbara Kingsolver, *Small Wonders* (New York: HarperCollins, 2002), 252.

Chapter 9. I Take Up the Way of Taking Only What Is Freely Given and Giving Freely of All That I Can
1. Henry Miller, *The Colossus of Maroussi* (New York: New Directions, 1941), 207.
2. Dorothea Hertzberg, "Aid to an American," *International Herald Tribune*, August 25, 2003. p. 6.

Chapter 10. I Take Up the Way of Engaging in Sexual Intimacy Respectfully and with an Open Heart
1. Sung-yuan Yu-Lu, *Dainihon Zoku Zokyo*, vol. 121, as

quoted in John Stevens, *Lust for Enlightenment: Buddhism and Sex* (Boston: Shambhala Publications, 1990), 91.

2. Ralph Waldo Emerson, "The Conduct of Life" (1860), in *Essays & Lectures* (New York: The Library of America, 1983), 1016.

3. John Cheever, *The Journals of John Cheever,* ed. Robert Gottlieb (New York: Knopf, 1991), 89.

4. Adapted from notes I took when attending a Stephen Wolinsky workshop on Quantum Psychology in Palo Alto, California, in 1998.

Chapter 11. I Take Up the Way of Letting Go of Anger

1. Stephen Levine, *Healing into Life and Death* (New York: Anchor Press, 1987), 228.

Chapter 12. I Take Up the Way of Supporting Life

1. Václav Havel, "The Future of Hope," in *The Art of the Impossible: Politics as Morality in Practice* (New York: Fromm International, 1998), 239.

2. Diane Ackerman, *A Slender Thread* (New York: Vintage Books, 1998), 243–4.